Ahab

INTERFACES

Series Editor: Barbara Green, O.P.

Ahab

The Construction of a King

Jerome T. Walsh

A Michael Glazier Book

LITURGICAL PRESS
Collegeville, Minnesota

www.litpress.org

A Michael Glazier Book published by Liturgical Press

Cover design by Ann Blattner. Watercolor by Ethel Boyle.

ISBN 13: 978-0-8146-5176-6
ISBN 10: 0-8146-5176-3

1	2	3	4	5	6	7	8

Library of Congress Cataloging-in-Publication Data

Walsh, Jerome T., 1942–
  Ahab : the construction of a king / Jerome T. Walsh.
    p. cm. — (Interfaces)
  Includes bibliographical references and index.
  ISBN 0-8146-5176-3 (alk. paper)
    1. Ahab, King of Israel.   2. Bible. O.T. Kings, 1st, XVI, 29-XXII,
  40—Criticism, interpretation, etc.   I. Title.   II. Series: Interfaces
  (Collegeville, Minn.)

  BS580.A5W35 2006
  222'.53'092—dc22   2005022641

Alex
1966–2002
ṣar-lî ʿâlêkā dôdî nāʿamtā llî mĕʾōd

CONTENTS

PREFACE

The book you hold in your hand is one of seventeen volumes in a set. This series, called INTERFACES, is a curriculum adventure, a creative opportunity in teaching and learning, presented at this moment in the long story of how the Bible has been studied, interpreted and appropriated.

The INTERFACES project was prompted by a number of experiences which you, perhaps, share. When I first taught undergraduates, the college had just received a substantial grant from the National Endowment for the Humanities, and one of the recurring courses designed within the grant was called Great Figures in Pursuit of Excellence. Three courses would be taught, each centering on a figure from some academic discipline or other, with a common seminar section to provide occasion for some integration. Some triads were more successful than others, as you might imagine. But the opportunity to concentrate on a single individual—whether historical or literary—to team teach, to make links to another pair of figures, and to learn new things about other disciplines was stimulating and fun for all involved. A second experience that gave rise to this series came at the same time, connected as well with undergraduates. It was my frequent experience to have Roman Catholic students feel quite put out about taking "more" biblical studies, since, as they confidently affirmed, they had already been there many times and done it all. That was, of course, not true; as we well know, there is always more to learn. And often those who felt most informed were the least likely to take on new information when offered it.

A stimulus as primary as my experience with students was the familiarity of listening to friends and colleagues at professional meetings talking about the research that excites us most. I often wondered: Do her undergraduate students know about this? Or how does he bring these ideas—clearly so energizing to him—into the college classroom? Perhaps some of us have felt bored with classes that seem wholly unrelated to research, that rehash the same familiar material repeatedly. Hence the idea for this series of books to bring to the fore and combine some of our research interests with our teaching and learning. Accordingly, this series is not so much about creating texts *for* student audiences but rather about *sharing* our scholarly passions with them. Because these volumes are intended each as a piece of original scholarship, they are geared to be stimulating to both students and established scholars, perhaps resulting in some fruitful collaborative learning adventures.

The series also developed from a widely shared sense that all academic fields are expanding and exploding, and that to contemplate "covering" even a testament (let alone the whole Bible or western monotheistic religions) needs to be abandoned in favor of something with greater depth and fresh focus. At the same time, the links between our fields are becoming increasingly obvious as well, and the possibilities for study which draw together academic realms that had once seemed separate are exciting. Finally, the spark of enthusiasm that almost always ignited when I mentioned to students and colleagues the idea of single figures in combination—interfacing—encouraged me that this was an idea worth trying.

And so with the leadership and help of the Liturgical Press's Academic Editor Linda Maloney, as well as with the encouragement and support of Editorial Director Mark Twomey, the series began to take shape.

Each volume in the INTERFACES series focuses clearly on a biblical character (or perhaps a pair of them). The characters from the first set of volumes are in some cases powerful—King Saul, Pontius Pilate—and familiar—John the Baptist, Jeremiah; in other cases they will strike you as minor and little-known—the Cannibal Mothers, Herodias. The second "litter" I added notables of various ranks and classes: Jezebel, queen of the Northern Israelite realm, James of Jerusalem and "brother of the Lord"; Simon the Pharisee, dinner host to Jesus; Legion, the Gerasene demoniac encountered so dramatically by Jesus. In this third set we find a similar contrast between apparently mighty and marginal characters: Jezebel's husband Ahab, king of Israel, the prophet Jonah who speaks a few powerfully efficacious words, and ben Sira, sage in late second temple Judah; less powerful but perhaps an even greater reading challenge stand Jephthah's daughter and Ezekiel's wife. A fourth set of characters includes Ahab, king of Israel; Jeremiah, prophet of Judah's exilic experience; and proto-apostle, Peter. In any case, each of them has been chosen to open up a set of worlds for consideration. The named (or unnamed) character interfaces with his or her historical-cultural world and its many issues, with other characters from biblical literature; each character has drawn forth the creativity of the author, who has taken on the challenge of engaging many readers. The books are designed for college students (though we think suitable for seminary courses and for serious Bible study), planned to provide young adults with relevant information and at a level of critical sophistication that matches the rest of the undergraduate curriculum.

In fact, the expectation is that what students are learning in other classes of historiography, literary theory, and cultural anthropology will find an echo in these books, each of which is explicit about at least two relevant methodologies. It is surely the case that biblical studies is in a methodology-conscious moment, and the INTERFACES series embraces it enthusiastically. Our hope is for students to continue to see the relationship between their best questions and their most valuable insights, between how they approach texts and what they find there. The volumes go well beyond familiar paraphrase of narratives to ask questions that are relevant in our era. At the same time, the series authors also have each dealt with the notion of the Bible as Scripture in a way condign for them. None of the books is preachy or hortatory, and yet the self-implicating aspects of working with the revelatory text are handled frankly. The assumption is, again, that college can be a good time for people to re-examine and rethink their beliefs and assumptions, and they need to do so in good company.

The INTERFACES volumes all challenge teachers to revision radically the scope of a course, to allow the many connections among characters to serve as its warp and weft. What would emerge fresh if a Deuteronomistic History class were organized around King Saul, Queen Jezebel, and/or her husband, Ahab, and the two women who petitioned their nameless monarch? How is Jesus' ministry thrown into fresh relief when structured by shared concerns implied by a demoniac, a Pharisee, James—a disciple—and John the Baptist—a mentor? What can be seen fresh when Peter joins the group? And for those who must "do it all" in one semester, a study of Genesis' Joseph, Herodias and Pontius Pilate might allow for a timely foray into postcolonialism. With whom would you now place the long-suffering but doughty wife of Ezekiel: with the able Jezebel, or with the apparently-celibate Jonah? Or perhaps with Herodias? Would Jephthah's daughter organize an excellent course with the Cannibal Mothers, and perhaps as well with the Gerasene demoniac, as fresh and under-heard voices speak their words to the powerful? Would you study monarchy effectively by working with bluebloods Ahab and Saul, as they contend with their opponents, whether John the Baptist or Pontius Pilate? Where would you place the indomitable Jeremiah? Depending on the needs of your courses and students, these rich and diverse character studies will offer you many options.

The INTERFACES volumes are not substitutes for the Bible. In every case, they are to be read with the text. Quoting has been kept to a minimum, for that very reason. The series is accompanied by a straightforward companion, *From Earth's Creation to John's Revelation: The INTERFACES Biblical Storyline Companion,* which provides an overview of the whole storyline into which the characters under special study fit. The companion is available gratis for those using two or more of the INTERFACES volumes. Already readers of diverse proficiency and familiarity have registered satisfaction with this slim overview narrated by biblical Sophia.

The series challenge—for publisher, writers, teachers, and students—is to combine the volumes creatively, to INTERFACE them well so that the vast potential of the biblical text continues to unfold for us all. These volumes offer a foretaste of other volumes currently on the drawing board. It has been a pleasure to work with the authors of these first volumes as well as with the series consultants: Carleen Mandolfo for Hebrew Bible and Catherine Murphy for New Testament. It is the hope of all of us that you will find the series useful and stimulating for your own teaching and learning.

Barbara Green, O.P.
INTERFACES Series Editor
May 16, 2005
Berkeley, California

INTRODUCTION

The greater part of the Bible is narrative prose. The entire first half of the Hebrew Bible is a single, almost unbroken narrative stretching from the beginnings of creation (Gen 1:1) to a time during the Babylonian Exile (2 Kgs 25:27-30 is set in "the thirty-seventh year of the exile of Jehoiachin," which was 560 B.C.E.). The first half of the New Testament comprises four separate, overlapping narrative accounts of the life and ministry of Jesus of Nazareth.

One of the central concerns of modern biblical studies has always been to extract from those narratives information about what lies behind them, in order to reconstruct the historical people and events at the origins of the text. To that end, critical biblical studies[1] has over the years developed several methods of analysis that enable the biblical scholar to undertake this sort of reconstruction. Those methods were fine-tuned during the nineteenth and twentieth centuries, and for the major part of the twentieth century dominated critical biblical scholarship to the virtual exclusion of any other approaches.

In the last decades of the twentieth century, however, some scholars began to raise new questions of the biblical text—questions that did not have the reconstruction of history as their focus. At times these questions were inspired by interest in the text's artistic (i.e., literary) qualities; at other times they were precipitated by concern for the effects the text has on issues of pressing contemporary concern (like human rights, genocide, or ecology). New questions required new analytical methods, and the last forty years or so have seen a proliferation of new critical approaches to biblical interpretation (often drawn from other academic disciplines such as literary criticism, social analysis, etc.). The result has been a lengthy period of experimentation and methodological ferment that has thrown the field into what might best be described as a happy chaos.

---

[1] "'Critical' biblical studies" does not mean, of course, study that "criticizes" the biblical text in a negative sense. In this context "criticism" is used positively, as in literary criticism or film criticism: it is reasoned analysis based on evidence and argumentation.

There are signs that the excitement of this experimentation is meta-morphosing into a new maturity. Students of the Bible are attempting to impose a level of discipline on some of the more extravagant ways of wielding the new methods, to adjudicate some of the more outré conclusions they have reached, and to lay out some ground rules for their responsible practice. One of the ways to determine the proper domains and purviews of the various interpretive approaches is by careful comparison of how different methods operate and what sorts of conclusions they reach.

It is in this spirit that we will undertake our investigations of Ahab, who was king of Israel in the second quarter of the ninth century B.C.E. Two principal questions will occupy us. First, a narrative critical question: How does the text depict Ahab? In other words, Ahab the *narrative character*—what is he like? Second, a historical critical question: How has the portrayal found in our texts grown and changed as it has been passed on from generation to generation? In other words, how much of Ahab's *historical character* has survived in the narrative character, and how much of the latter is the product of later elaboration?

The story of King Ahab begins in 1 Kings 16:29 and ends in 1 Kings 22:40. His presence in these six chapters is quite uneven. In chapters 20–22, for instance, he is the central character; by contrast, in chapters 17–19 Elijah is much more prominent than Ahab. In fact, in chapters 17 and 19 Ahab appears in only two verses. Nevertheless, almost no other king after Solomon merits a regnal account of such length.

We will begin with a brief presentation of the Ahab of history (Part One). The information a responsible investigation of the historical evidence can deem reliable is meager in the extreme, and the resultant portrait of Ahab will be sketchy indeed. It will supply, however, a benchmark for comparison for the other two, longer parts of the book. Part Two will examine the texts as we have them to bring into relief Ahab as he is portrayed by the narrative. It is not surprising that, given much more data to work with, our picture of the Ahab of narrative will be much more complex and detailed than that of the Ahab of history. What *is* surprising is the almost total lack of resemblance between the two. And so, in Part Three, we will attempt to reconstruct the history of the *texts* about Ahab, to determine how his textual portrait developed over time and whether any of the traits we find in the Ahab of narrative can plausibly be considered original to the Ahab of history.

I am grateful to many whose personal friendship has sustained me during the writing of this book and whose professional support has contributed to its betterment. I am particularly grateful to Dr. Johanna Stiebert, of the University of Tennessee at Knoxville, for intercontinental constancy; to Dr. Barbara Green, of the Dominican School of Philosophy and Theology, for able advice and incisive editing; and to Dr. Mark Goodwin and Dr. Brian Schmisek of the University of Dallas, through whose careful reading this book has gained considerably in clarity. For the flaws that remain, I claim sole credit.

All quotations from the biblical text are taken from the New Revised Standard Version, unless otherwise noted.

PART ONE
The Ahab of History

THE AHAB OF HISTORY

The historian's task of reconstructing a figure of the ancient past is a bit like that of the paleontologist who tries to discern the shape, size, and stance of an unknown species of dinosaur from a toe, a tooth, and a broken vertebra. The evidence is sparse to the point of despair, often ambiguous (are the toe and the tooth even from the same animal?), and can be glued together only with massive amounts of interpretation and conjecture.

The first step in the procedure is to amass the evidence. For historical reconstruction, primary evidence is of two types, both of which should ideally be contemporary or near contemporary to the ancient context. Written records are, of course, invaluable but, unfortunately, rare. Unwritten remains—art, architecture, artifacts—can also shed light on a society and on the people and events that may have marked its life. Neither sort of evidence, however, can be accepted uncritically. Even at their most reliable and insightful, written records always reflect the point of view of their creators, with the limitations and biases that implies. And unwritten materials, by their very muteness, require interpretation regarding date, context, implications, and significance. Does the discovery of an Egyptian statue in Israel, for instance, attest to international trade relations or to an Egyptian military incursion?

And so the second step of historical reconstruction is the process of interpretation (historians call this the "art of historical inference"). Evidence, written and unwritten, must be interpreted, usually in the light of other equally ambiguous pieces of evidence. Such a procedure is, inevitably, circular. Furthermore, filling in the gaps between the scattered pieces of evidence—connecting the toe with the tooth, so to speak—is unavoidably speculative. Certainty is never assured, and the most that one can reasonably hope for is plausibility. The more comprehensively and consistently an interpretation accounts for the available evidence, the more conviction it will carry.

Amassing the Evidence—Written Records

Contemporary and near-contemporary written records for ancient Israelite history are scarce in the extreme. This often comes as a surprise to the student, since so much of the Old Testament text presents itself as historical accounts. The key word, of course, is the qualifier "contemporary." Our biblical knowledge of King Ahab derives from 1 Kings, which forms part of what scholars call the "Deuteronomic History" (comprising Joshua, Judges, 1–2 Samuel, and 1–2 Kings). The composition history of this massive work remains a matter of debate, but most scholars would not date its earliest edition before the late seventh century B.C.E., more than two centuries after Ahab's death. No doubt the Deuteronomic Historian incorporated earlier material in his narrative. Discerning that earlier material, however, and extracting it from the Deuteronomic Historian's interpretive use of it constitute no easy task. This is the agenda of source and redaction criticism, which will occupy our attention later on. For the time being we will make use only of the limited biblical data that redaction critics generally ascribe to the oldest pre-Deuteronomic sources.

Ahab's father, King Omri, is credited with a coup d'état that overthrew the ruling dynasty in Israel in the early ninth century B.C.E. (1 Kgs 16:21-23). After four years of civil war he consolidated his power over the kingdom and, in the seven or eight years remaining to him, undertook a policy of alliance-building with neighboring states, notably Judah to the south and Tyre to the north. Alliances were cemented by marriage: Omri wed his son, Ahab, to the daughter of the king of Tyre, and his daughter, Athaliah,[1] to the crown prince of Judah. Midway through his reign Omri also founded and began to fortify a new capital, called Samaria, on what had once been a privately-owned hill. Short as it was, Omri's reign seems to have brought Israel onto the world stage. Long afterwards, Assyrian records refer to Israel as the "land of Omri" and its king as the "son of Omri."[2]

---

[1] Whether Athaliah was Omri's daughter or granddaughter is uncertain: 2 Kings 8:18 calls Athaliah the "daughter of Ahab," while 8:26 calls her the "daughter of Omri," which might, in Hebrew, mean simply "female descendant." (This is why the *NRSV* renders the phrase "granddaughter of Omri" in 8:26.) Chronologically either seems possible. Whichever is the case, the marriage cemented diplomatic relations between the kingdoms of Israel and Judah.

[2] An inscription of the Assyrian emperor Adad-nirari III from the late ninth or early eighth century B.C.E. speaks of the "country of Omri." Paradoxically, the Black Obelisk of Shalmaneser III (from the 840s B.C.E.) calls King Jehu of Israel, the usurper who wiped out the entire descendance of Ahab (2 Kings 9–10), the "son of Omri." Brad Kelle argues that the use of "Omri" in reference to Jehu need not be a genealogical error on Shalmaneser's part but may only indicate that "House of Omri" was the Assyrian name for the country of Israel. See "What's in a Name: Neo-Assyrian Designations for the Northern Kingdom and

Ahab and his father Omri are in fact the first Israelite kings for whom we have any *contemporary* written evidence. Three ancient Near Eastern texts, all ninth-century royal inscriptions by non-Israelite rulers, mention these kings. The most important is the so-called "Monolith Inscription," Assyrian emperor Shalmaneser III's account of a battle he fought against a coalition of small west Asian states at Qarqar in western Syria in 853 B.C.E., just prior to Ahab's death. (The Old Testament makes no reference to this battle.) The monument, discovered in the 1840s, recounts Shalmaneser's claims of a "victory" (which modern historians are persuaded was a stalemate, at best), and enumerates the enemy forces he claims to have overcome. Leading the coalition was Hadad-ezer of Damascus, with 1,200 chariots, 1,200 cavalry, and 20,000 infantry. The second most important coalition member seems to have been "Ahab the Israelite," with 2,000 chariots and 10,000 infantry.[3] (Apparently the Israelite military had not yet developed to include mounted soldiery.)

The second contemporary inscription, known as the "Mesha Stele" or the "Moabite Stone," was discovered in 1868. It commemorates a victory over Israelite control by King Mesha of Moab. (The Bible makes passing references to Mesha's rebellion in 2 Kings 1:1 and 3:4-5.) Mesha tells us that "Omri . . . humbled Moab" for a long time, and that he "occupied the land of Medeba . . . in his time and half the time of his son(s), forty years."[4] He also says that "the king of Israel" built two cities in Moabite territory,

---

Their Implications for Israelite History and Biblical Interpretation," *Journal of Biblical Literature* 121 (2002) 639–66, esp. pp. 641–51. Alternatively, Tammi Schneider proposes that Jehu may indeed have been a descendant of Omri, but not through the line of Ahab. See "Did King Jehu Kill His Own Family? New Interpretation Reconciles Biblical Text with Famous Assyrian Inscription," *Biblical Archaeology Review* 21 (1995) 26-33, 80.

[3] Some scholars dispute this interpretation. They claim that Assyria itself would not have had more than 2,000 chariots at this time, and that the unreliable orthography of the Monolith Inscription allows the surmise that Ahab's "2,000" is an error for "200." They point to another inscription in which Shalmaneser commemorates the same battle, where he names Hadad-ezer of Damascus and Irhuleni of Hamath ("700 chariots, 700 cavalry, and 10,000 infantry") but does not mention Ahab of Israel. They conclude that Hadad-ezer and Irhuleni were the leaders of the coalition, and Ahab was but a minor partner. (See the discussion in Gösta W. Ahlström, *The History of Ancient Palestine* [Minneapolis: Fortress, 1993] 577–78.) I will assume the majority view that the Monolith Inscription's figure is accurate and that Ahab was a leader of the coalition.

[4] The figure "forty years" is a conventional term for a generation; it is unlikely to be meant literally. There are two unresolved translation difficulties in this passage. First, the Moabite meaning of the word *ḥṣy* is disputed; does it mean "half," as it does in Hebrew, or one of several other proposals (e.g., "sum") that have been offered? Second, is the word "son(s)" to be read as singular or plural? The text permits either reading, and therefore could refer to Ahab alone or to him along with one or both of his successor-sons, Omri's grand-

Ataroth and Jahaz, and that "he dwelt there [in Jahaz] while he was fighting against me." Both of these sites are located deep in traditionally Moabite territory, east of the Dead Sea. They probably represent border fortresses at the extremes of Israelite expansionism in Transjordan. The information is difficult to interpret, given the ambiguities of the text and the avoidance of naming any king(s) of Israel except Omri. The Bible dates Mesha's rebellion to coincide with the death of Ahab. This is reasonable, since Israelite military strength may have been depleted by the battle against Shalmaneser III that had just occurred at Qarqar. Moreover, the inherent instability when a throne changes hands lays a country open to insurrection, and Ahab's own death was followed only a year or so later by the death of his son and successor, Ahaziah. A plausible reconstruction of events, then, would be that Omri's diplomatic alliances with Judah to the south and Tyre to the north permitted aggressive policies eastward in Transjordan—probably in competition with Aramean forces from Damascus—and that this resulted in Israelite occupation of Moabite territory and the establishment of border fortresses. Ahab's reign would have seen the continuation and consolidation of Omri's expansionist undertakings. The battle of Qarqar and two royal deaths in quick succession gave Moab an opportunity to throw off the Israelite yoke in the years immediately following Ahab's reign, either during the brief reign of the unfortunate Ahaziah or that of his brother Jehoram.

The third contemporary inscription was discovered at Tel Dan, in northern Israel, in 1993; it is often called the "House of David" inscription. It celebrates a victory of Hazael of Damascus over the rulers of both Israelite kingdoms sometime in the second half of the ninth century B.C.E.[5] The relevant part of the inscription is frustratingly lacking in legible proper names, but there is a scholarly consensus about conjectural restoration. The text reads, in part,

[   ]ram son of [   ] king of Israel, and [ ] killed [   ]iahu son of
[   ]g of the house of David. And I set [   ]
their land into [   ].

---

sons. On the translation difficulties of the inscription see Kent P. Jackson, "The Language of the Mesha Inscription," *Studies in the Mesha Inscription and Moab*, ed. J. Andrew Dearman (Atlanta: Scholars Press, 1989) 96–130. On the difficulties of historical reconstruction see J. Andrew Dearman, "Historical Reconstruction and the Mesha Inscription," in the same volume, pp. 155–210.

[5] For this Hazael of Damascus see the story of Elisha's instigation of Hazael's seizure of the throne of Damascus by assassinating Ben-hadad (2 Kgs 8:7-15). According to 2 Kings 9:1-13 Elisha was also responsible for the coup d'état of Jehu, to whom the Old Testament imputes the royal murders that the Tel Dan inscription ascribes to Hazael (see 2 Kgs 9:14-28).

The original discoverers of the inscription proposed this restoration:

> [I killed Jeho]ram son of [Ahab] king of Israel, and [I] killed [Ahaz]iahu son of [Jehoram kin]g of the house of David. And I set [their towns into ruins and turned] their land into [desolation].[6]

This gives us little information about Ahab himself, particularly in view of the fact that his name is lacking and must be supplied conjecturally. It does suggest, however, that any alliance between Israel and Damascus that may have figured in the battle of Qarqar did not long survive Ahab's death.

Amassing the Evidence—Archaeological Remains

Archaeology in Israel has been immensely productive. Since the nineteenth century numerous sites have yielded a vast store of information about the material cultures of the peoples of the region from the Stone Age to the Islamic period and beyond. Given the religious impetus that energized and funded most early archaeological campaigns in the Syro-Palestinian environment, it is not surprising that the most intense focus has been on material and periods that illuminate our understanding of biblical history and the biblical text. The Omrid period in the ninth century B.C.E. is a case in point. Perhaps the most important site for our understanding of this period is Samaria itself. According to 1 Kings it was founded by Omri, and therefore has no significant occupational prehistory. This has been confirmed archaeologically, with only scant traces of human occupation found below the earliest Israelite strata. These earliest strata can be confidently attributed to Omri and/or Ahab. Beyond Samaria several sites have revealed impressive architecture and engineering that date to the same reigns. There is little doubt that the decades of Ahab's kingship were a time of impressive material prosperity and growth.

Samaria was first excavated by Harvard archaeologists in the early twentieth century and by a Joint Expedition of five institutions in the 1930s. Among the important finds datable to the period of Omri and Ahab are monumental walls and buildings as well as exquisite decorative items. Omri fortified the palace area of his capital with a single wall built of dressed stones laid dry (without mortar). The wall is 1.6 meters thick and encircles the summit of the hill on which the royal compound was situated.

---

[6] Avraham Biran and Joseph Naveh, "An Aramaic Stele Fragment from Tel Dan," *Israel Exploration Journal* 43 (1993) 81–98, and "The Tel Dan Inscription: A New Fragment," *Israel Exploration Journal* 45 (1995) 1–18.

Ahab improved the strength of the defensive fortifications considerably. He expanded the area and built a much stronger casemate wall ten meters thick. The increased size and casemate design of the wall were necessary because it served as a retaining wall surrounding thousands of tons of fill used to enlarge the hill in order to accommodate the royal and administrative complex atop it.[7] The palace area itself yielded some of the finest decorative ivory artifacts ever found in Israel. Most are plaques carved in relief; they were probably adornments inlaid into furniture, walls, or the like. A few are sculptures in the round. The elegant carving is a mixture of Egyptian and Phoenician styles, perhaps reflecting the Phoenician alliances of the Omrids. Most of the ivories were scattered throughout the royal enclosure in contexts that are impossible to date securely. Experts separate them into two groups, tentatively dated to the ninth (Omri and Ahab) and eighth (Jeroboam II) centuries respectively. There are striking biblical correlations for the finds: Ahab is said to have built an "ivory house" (1 Kgs 22:39)—presumably a palace famous for its ivory decorations—and, a century later, Amos announces the destruction of the "houses of ivory" of the wealthy of Bethel (Amos 3:15) and excoriates those who loll on "beds of ivory" (6:4). Even if the ivories found at Samaria are not themselves from Ahab's palace, they illustrate vividly the sophisticated artistry that characterized Samaria and Israel at its finest.

Omrid architecture and engineering were not confined to Samaria. Monumental buildings, casemate retaining walls around expanded royal enclosures, huge six-chambered gate complexes, dry-laid ashlar construction, and other architectural echoes of Samaria appear at Megiddo, Gezer, Hazor, Jezreel, and elsewhere and attest to the energy and creativity of the Omrid dynasty. It is likely that much of this activity is to be dated, at least in its inception, to Ahab's reign.[8]

---

[7] A "casemate" wall consists of an outer wall separated from an inner wall by open space. The outer and inner walls are joined by connecting partitions that divide the intervening space into a series of chambers that can be used for storage or the like. Ahab's casemate wall at Samaria had a two-meter outer wall, a one-meter inner wall, and narrow interior chambers seven meters long. Instead of using them as storage rooms Ahab seems to have filled the casemates with packed earth to bolster the wall's function as a retaining wall.

[8] Several archaeologists have dated the astounding engineering of the water systems at Megiddo and Hazor to the Omrids as well. Recently, however, this dating has been challenged in favor of an eighth-century provenance. On the architectural accomplishments of the Omrids see Israel Finkelstein and Neil Asher Silberman, *The Bible Unearthed: Archaeology's New Vision of Ancient Israel and the Origin of Its Sacred Texts* (New York: Simon and Schuster, 2001) 168–95.

Conclusion—the Historical Ahab

The evidence points clearly to the pivotal importance of Omri and Ahab in the history of Israel. Omri seems to have been responsible for the emergence of a stable and powerful political force in the country.[9] His diplomatic and military accomplishments ushered in a period of internal stability and external expansion, of material prosperity and international commerce, that made Israel a force to be reckoned with in the larger world.

Given the brevity of Omri's reign, it fell to his son Ahab to consolidate and capitalize on Omri's initiatives. All the evidence points to his success in doing so. He maintained positive diplomatic relations with Phoenicia and Judah and, at least at the end of his reign, with Damascus. His military strength kept Moab under his sway and assured the west Asian coalition's ability to withstand Assyrian aggression. The grandeur of the building projects that characterize Ahab's tenure indicates impressive technological innovation and accomplishment, international traffic in goods and ideas, and high standards of art and luxury.

The limitations of our evidence, of course, do not permit us to infer anything about how widely this happy state of affairs extended to the general populace. A luxurious lifestyle for the upper classes does not necessarily mean widespread prosperity; it can just as easily be built on the backs of the oppressed.

Beyond this, any attempt to flesh out the skeleton of Ahab's character must draw from and build on the portrait in the biblical text. However, as we have seen, the biblical portrait is not "contemporary or near-contemporary," and, as we shall see, its depiction of Ahab is strikingly different from what we have just sketched. In order to appreciate just *how* different it is we turn to narrative criticism and its techniques for understanding the ways characters are brought to life in narratives.

---

[9] This is true whether one hews fairly closely to the biblical record or accepts the more skeptical reconstructions of many contemporary historians. In the former case the wreckage of the United Monarchy after the death of Solomon left the northern part of the country vulnerable to violence and almost continuous political turmoil. In the fifty years between Solomon's death and Omri's coup Israel endured five kings, two seizures of the throne by assassination, one royal suicide, and a civil war. In the latter case Omri was the first to unify the disparate tribal, religious, and ethnic groups of the northern part of Palestine into a single nation.

PART TWO
The Ahab of Narrative

CHAPTER ONE

First Impressions

Narrative Criticism 1

The Reader and the Narrative World

Study of a narrative character has unexpected parallels to study of a historical figure. The key to understanding this convergence is the concept of "narrative world." In composing a narrative text an author creates a circumscribed world out of words. Within that world a narrator tells a story to a listener (technically called the "narratee"). The story, in turn, is inhabited by characters and the events in which they are involved. This "narrative world" is in several ways analogous to the daily world in which we live, where we learn about historical people and events from the testimony of others.

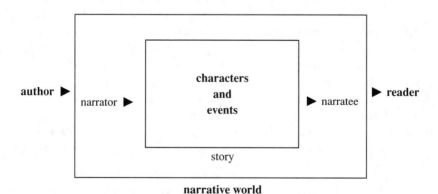

(Adapted from Terence J. Keegan, *Interpreting the Bible: A Popular Introduction to Biblical Hermeneutics* [New York: Paulist, 1985] 94.)

In terms of this diagram the reader's role is complex. Since the story is told not to the reader by the author, but to the narratee by the narrator, the reader—you or I—will receive the story appropriately only to the degree that we manage to identify ourselves with the narratee—that is, to the degree that we enter the narrative world ourselves. Literary critics sometimes call this the "willing suspension of disbelief"—though J. R. R. Tolkien more perceptively speaks of "secondary belief": a positive attitude rather than a doubly negative one.[1] Tolkien's positive approach is warranted. Reading narrative is not simply a matter of staving off skepticism; once we succeed in entering the narrative world we tend to respond to events and characters in the same way we do to events and people in the primary world of the everyday.

Yet in the final analysis there will always be a gap between the ideal narratee and ourselves. On the one hand, the narrator has expectations of the narratee that we cannot meet. Old Testament narratives, for instance, are told in ancient Hebrew, and few of us are natively fluent in that language; unlike the ideal narratee, we need the help of linguists and translators. On the other hand, we have cultural backgrounds, not to mention individual life histories, that differ from those of an ideal narratee and will inevitably affect and effect the way we hear and respond to the story.

One implication of the gap between ideal narratee and real reader is that each reader's experience of a text will be unique. Not that different readers will have totally different experiences—there is a commonality to human beings that assures a generally consistent response to a fixed text— but the unique history that each of us brings to the text will nuance the ways in which we respond to the characters and events of the narrative world. Furthermore, as we shall see later, narrators do not spell everything out, and their reticence offers readers the opportunity to fill gaps in different ways. This is another source of variation in the reception of texts by readers. (This is analogous to the necessity of *interpretation* in the recovery of a historical character: The incompleteness and ambiguity of the evidence allow for a variety of persuasive and consistent historical reconstructions.)

Beyond identifying with the narratee, however, the *critical* reader has an additional task. He or she seeks to understand not only *what* the story is saying but also *how* the story is saying it. In other words, the critical reader is interested both in responding to the story and in discovering the narrative

---

[1] J. R. R. Tolkien, "Tree and Leaf," *The Tolkien Reader* (New York: Ballantine Books, 1966) 37 (paginated separately). "Tree and Leaf" combines an essay, "On Fairy Stories," which Tolkien originally presented as an Andrew Lang Lecture at the University of St. Andrews in 1938, with a related story, "Leaf by Niggle." Both were originally (and separately) published in 1947.

techniques by which the story is eliciting those responses. And so the critical reader must put one foot, so to speak, in the narratee's shoes but keep the other foot *outside* the narrative world. Critical reading then is a dialectical process of responding to the story as we receive it, attending to our own responses, and returning to the text to identify what it is in the text that is evoking that response from us.

It should not surprise us, then, that one reader's understanding of a text—the significance of its events, the assessment of its characters, the often tacit causal matrix that unifies it—will differ in details from another's. Criteria of comprehensiveness, coherence, and plausibility are as applicable here as in historical reconstruction. To what degree does a particular reading of a narrative account for all the data of the text? To what extent does the reading reveal a narrative world that makes sense: events that are linked by plausible cause and effect, characters that act believably and according to consistent values? These are criteria of *persuasiveness* rather than of *correctness,* and they lead to judgments about whether or not a given reading is *adequate* to the text, not to whether or not it is the "right" reading. Literary criticism in general has long been suspicious of using a presumed "author's intention" as a criterion for interpretation. *A fortiori* in reading ancient texts, where we have no access to an author's mind other than the text itself, the claim to have identified an author's intention, and thereby to have discerned the "right" interpretation of a text, seems particularly presumptuous.

The coherence and consistency of the narrative world are independent of its direct relationship to the world we live in. The narrative world subsists on its own terms. Fantasy, for instance, unfolds in a narrative world where magic works, where dragons or dwarfs may dwell, or where animals may talk. More "realistic" narrative may display a world where people and events are much like those in our own lived experience, though they do not, and never did, exist—the Pequod, Captain Ahab, and his white whale, for instance. Even history writing can be understood this way: It too creates a narrative, and a narrative world, out of words, but with the added claim that the people and events and relationships in that narrative world are congruent with the real world we live in. The quality of history writing *as history* depends on how accurately it reflects the real world (its "referentiality"), but its quality *as narrative*—indeed, *any* narrative's quality as narrative—depends solely on the coherence of the narrative world created by the author. To enter the narrative world satisfactorily, the reader must endeavor to accept it on its terms. One's disappointment in a particular narrative can usually be traced either to the narrative's failure to be faithful to its own terms or to the reader's inability to be comfortable with them. Once we have entered that world, however, the story we hear from the narrator is a *real* story, about people who are real and events that matter.

The Narrator and the Reader

To identify with a narratee is to sit at the feet of a narrator. Narrators, particularly biblical narrators, are elusive beings. They tend to transparency—which is why we often confuse them with authors. Fundamentally, the narrator is the voice that tells us the story. Even when the narrator seems to disappear into the impersonality of the recital, he is audible: The story comes to us in his words. That is to say, the narrator is an active inhabitant of the narrative world, and therefore, like everything else in the narrative world, he is a creation of the author. The narrator's unobtrusiveness can be misleading. We are inclined to overlook him and treat his story as disembodied words, but the narrator is the author's access to us and to our responses.

In much modern literature "narrator" is a highly problematic category. In theory an author is not obliged to create a narrator in the author's own image and likeness. And in practice modern authors have experimented with insane narrators, lying narrators, multiple narrators with cross-purposes and contrasting value systems, and every other imaginable variation.[2] In the view of most biblical scholars, biblical narrators are much better behaved. The story they tell is a reliable representation of characters and events in the narrative world, and the values they espouse and expound are coherent and, presumably, approximate those of the author.[3] Some biblical scholars, on the other hand, have begun to explore the possibility of a more complex and sophisticated use of the narrator in biblical narrative, particularly the interweaving of multiple narrative voices.[4] As an explana-

---

[2] One famous example of the danger of using a narrator who is at odds with the author is Daniel Defoe's essay, "The Shortest-Way With The Dissenters" (1702), an ironic anti-Tory pamphlet written from what appeared to be a pro-Tory viewpoint. Both sides in the debate missed Defoe's irony, and he was subsequently arrested, tried, fined, and pilloried for "seditious libel."

[3] This is not to say that a biblical narrator may not mislead or even deceive the narratee for specific purposes. We should not assume that either biblical authors or their narrators have as their first priority a plain, simple story line (whether historical or not). Narrative—including history writing—is meant to move, to persuade, to convince the hearer of the rightness of a particular view of things. Authors and their narrators do not always scruple in their means to that end.

[4] See, for example, the works of Robert Polzin, *Moses and the Deuteronomist: A Literary Study of the Deuteronomic History* (New York: Seabury, 1980); *Samuel and the Deuteronomist: A Literary Study of the Deuteronomic History* (New York: Harper & Row, 1989);

tion for contrasting value systems in a text, analysis in terms of multiple narrative voices would be a literary analogue to the historical-critical appeal to independent sources lying behind a composite text. When we consider the stories of Ahab in 1 Kings 20–22 we shall have occasion to discuss this approach in greater detail and to consider its advantages.

However, even when we deem a narrator omniscient and reliable, this does not mean he is "objective" or "neutral," any more than it means that the author held no opinions and made no value judgments. The biblical narrator is the author's entrée to the reader, and any author who wishes to shape his or her readers' responses (and what author doesn't?) must accomplish that goal through the instrumentality of the narrator. To put it simply, *narrators manipulate readers*. This is no bad thing. If the narrator does not evoke a response from us, our reading experience is flat and forgettable. A sense of satisfaction in reading means that we have been stimulated to a fulfilling emotional, intellectual, spiritual, even visceral response. This is no less true for the *critical* reader, though the critical reader, as I have already said, seeks to go beyond savoring the immediate experience and to identify *how* the narrator has elicited that response.

Narrators have at their disposal an enormous arsenal of techniques for affecting readers. This is not the place to present a comprehensive narrative poetics, but a single example may suffice to show how, and how powerfully, a narrator can arouse a response. "Point of view" is a complex aspect of narrative, but in its simplest form it means the position from which I, as reader, witness a narrative scene. The classic explanatory analogy is drawn from cinema. I can see only what the camera shows me. The position of the camera (and, by inference, the director's manipulation of that position) establishes the angle from which I see things as well as my distance from them. Both are significant. The angle of my view enables me to see certain things, but it leaves me ignorant of other things that are excluded from my field of vision. Furthermore, it can position me with respect to the characters by having me share one character's point of view or, conversely, by making me a neutral observer. Distance affects emotional intensity: A close-up of two characters arguing audibly will create much greater tension in me than a distance shot of angry gestures. Narrators manipulate point of view similarly, and to similar effect. When Solomon stands silently listening to the

---

and *David and the Deuteronomist: A Literary Study of the Deuteronomic History* (Bloomington: Indiana University Press, 1993). Drawing on the insights of Russian literary theorist Mikhail Bakhtin, Polzin explores the "polyphony" of voices that construct the narratives of Deuteronomy through 2 Samuel. (To this point, as far as I know, no one yet proposes that one or another biblical author has created a lying or insane narrator!)

two harlots present their case before him (1 Kgs 3:16-22) we sense ourselves standing next to him, seeing what he sees, hearing what he hears, and
worrying the same knotty problem he is stymied by. However, when he
says, "Bring me a sword!" (3:24), we are as taken aback as the two women
and suddenly find ourselves standing with them, staring at the king, and
wondering fearfully what this ominous command could possibly mean. And
finally when the narrator takes a long view and tells us of the Israelites' awe
at Solomon's judgment (3:28) we understand their reaction, and perhaps
even share it intellectually, but we don't *feel* it as intensely as we did
Solomon's puzzlement or the women's trepidation.

Narrators manipulate readers. We might say that it is an essential part
of their job description, and it is not something undesirable. Reading's goal
is to enter as fully as possible into the experience the narrator offers us, to
allow ourselves to be moved deeply and, potentially, transformed by it.
Narrative criticism's goal is to become aware of the manipulation and to
see how it was achieved—not in order to counteract it, which would do
nothing but eviscerate the reading experience, but to celebrate and admire
its skill and subtlety.

Characters and Characterization

Since the focus of this study is a particular biblical character it is
worthwhile spending some effort to understand how narrative texts create
characters and achieve characterization. Consider the paradox: Characters
in a story, like everything else in the narrative world, are built out of words.
How does it happen that a narrator can bring us to admire one set of words
and despise another set? Why do *these* words win our friendship and *those*
words our contempt? There are two interrelated aspects to the answer.
First, there are the ways in which the narrator presents us with information
about a character; second, there are the ways in which the narrator maneuvers us to collaborate actively in creating the character.

The narrator's most straightforward way of constructing a character is
simply to *tell* us something about the character. One common form of
telling is to use titles, or nouns in apposition. To call someone "*King* Ahab"
or "Elijah *the Tishbite*" is to tell us something about him (even if we aren't
sure what a "Tishbite" is!). The narrator can describe a physical or personality trait ("King David was *old*" [1 Kgs 1:1]; "Eglon was a *very fat man*"
[Judg 3:17]; "Obadiah *revered* the LORD *greatly*" [1 Kgs 18:3]). Or the narrator can describe a more transitory quality, like a mood, a motivation, or a
temporary condition (Ahab "set out toward home, *resentful and sullen*" [1
Kgs 20:43]; "when Solomon saw that [Jeroboam] was *industrious* he gave

him charge over all the forced labor of the house of Joseph" [1 Kgs 11:29]; the kings "were sitting on their thrones, *arrayed in their robes*" [1 Kgs 22:10]). This sort of description is relatively uncommon in biblical narrative—certainly much rarer than it is in contemporary fiction—and the described trait will usually play an important role in subsequent narrative development. The ancient reader would have been sensitive to the infrequency of description and would have taken its presence as significant. The other side of the coin, though, is that the explicitness of description leaves little need to infer anything beyond it. We respond to the description—perhaps with sympathy for David's age or admiration for Obadiah's devotion—but to know that King David is old, or that Obadiah is devout, does not impel us to speculate further about their character.

More powerful as a strategy of characterization is "showing": The narrator portrays a scene that *shows* us a character thinking,[5] speaking, or acting. This has two different results, both of which increase the reader's level of involvement with the character. First, it is closer to our lived experience than "telling" is. In everyday life we have no omniscient narrator to inform us about our fellows; we infer from others' speech and actions what they are truly like. To come to know characters in the narrative world in the same way is to engage that world as we do the everyday world. This increases the density, so to speak, of the narrative world and makes our experience of it seem more "real." Second, the tasks of inferring tacit motives and meanings from behavior and of basing judgments about personality traits and values on those inferences require us to become active collaborators with the narrator in creating the character. Was Ahab aware of Jezebel's machinations against Naboth or not (1 Kgs 21:1-16)? The narrator's silence permits either answer. If I conclude that he was, then I envision a figure who shrewdly anticipates, and perhaps even manipulates, his wife. If I conclude that he was not, then I envision a passive figure who has little control over the queen. In either case *my* judgment as reader contributes decisively to the character of the king.

More powerful still is what we might call "indirect showing." In this situation the narrator does not directly show me the character I am interested in but another character speaking or acting with regard to my character. In other words, what I learn about my character is mediated to me not by a reliable narrator but by one of the other characters, about whose reliability I may not be certain. As a reader, then, I must first ascertain the reliability of the character I see, and only then can I infer anything about

---

[5] Showing us a character's thoughts (technically called "internal monologue") enjoys some of the benefits of "telling" as well. Assuming the narrator is reliable, "telling" gives us reliable information about the character. Because we presume the character is not lying to himself, internal monologue is similarly reliable.

the character I am interested in. This technique too mirrors real life, since much of our knowledge of others comes from third-hand reports. My role in the process of characterization is even greater than with direct showing, since I am actively involved in the creation of *both* characters as well as the relationship between them. Consider for example Obadiah's claim that Ahab has been searching obsessively for Elijah since he announced the drought three years before (1 Kgs 18:10). The first question is whether to believe Obadiah or not. If we do, then we need to conjecture Ahab's motivation for the search: Does he seek Elijah to plead with him for the end of the drought, or to undertake repentance, or to kill the prophet? And if we do not believe Obadiah, does it imply anything about the king that his majordomo would slander him in this way?

King Ahab—First Impressions

The books of Kings have a characteristic way of recounting the reign of a king. The account begins with a stereotyped introduction that synchronizes the king's accession to the throne with the regnal year of the king in the other Israelite kingdom. Other details follow: the length of the king's reign, his capital city, and in the case of kings of Judah his age at accession and the name of his mother. This is followed by the narrator's theological evaluation of the king; all kings of Israel and many kings of Judah are condemned, some kings of Judah are approved with reservation, and only two kings (Hezekiah and Josiah) get unqualified praise. Next comes a brief remark about some noteworthy event of the reign; assassinations and incidents affecting the Temple in Jerusalem are frequent topics. The account then closes with another stereotyped formula that refers the reader to a source where further information can be found,[6] and details the death and burial of the king and the name of his successor.[7] This pattern begins with the account of Rehoboam's reign (1 Kgs 14:21-31)[8] and continues virtually unbroken

---

[6] Three different sources are named: the "Book of the Acts of Solomon" (1 Kgs 11:41), the "Book of the Annals of the Kings of Israel" *(passim)* and the "Book of the Annals of the Kings of Judah" (also *passim*). Sadly, none of these works is extant today, and their character and contents are matters of speculation.

[7] On the stereotyped regnal formulas see Jerome T. Walsh, *1 Kings,* Berit Olam: Studies in Biblical Hebrew Narrative and Poetry (Collegeville: Liturgical Press, 1996) 206–207. A more technical account appears in Burke O. Long, *1 Kings with an Introduction to Historical Literature,* The Forms of the Old Testament Literature 9 (Grand Rapids: Eerdmans, 1984) 160–61.

[8] There are similar concluding formulas before this (David, 1 Kings 2:10-11; Solomon, 1 Kings 11:41-43; Jeroboam I, 1 Kings 14:19-20), but none of these reigns has a formulaic introduction like the ones from Rehoboam's reign on.

through the remainder of 1 and 2 Kings. The concluding formula for one regnal account usually leads immediately into the introductory formula for the next; only rarely does any information fall between accounts.

The first observation a reader makes about the story of Ahab is its enormous length. Of the seven regnal accounts from Rehoboam to Omri, the longest, that of Asa of Judah, takes sixteen verses. By contrast, Ahab's regnal account begins at 1 Kings 16:29 and stretches to 1 Kings 22:40—a total of more than 230 verses. Where the preceding narratives recount a single event from each reign, the Ahab story incorporates six chapters of very diverse stories. It is thus clear from the outset that the narrator considers the reign of Ahab of momentous importance in his history of Israel. Yet, paradoxically, after the first few verses Ahab recedes into the background for three chapters before becoming central in chapters 20–22. The intervening three chapters focus on the prophet Elijah, who thereby becomes no less prominent a figure in Ahab's story than Ahab himself.

Our first impressions of Ahab come to us directly from the narrator. Of Ahab's background we know that his father, a military leader, had seized the throne with the support of his troops (1 Kgs 16:16, 21-22). Beyond that we learn little more than that Omri, like all Israelite kings before him, supported the cult of the golden calves at the sanctuaries Jeroboam I had established at Dan and Bethel (the "way of Jeroboam," as 16:26 puts it). Of Ahab himself we learn that he will reign much longer than his father and that he will reign from the capital city his father built (16:29; cf. 16:24).

The narrator's theological evaluation of Ahab is much more elaborate than usual. Omri, for instance, was condemned as "more evil than all who were before him," and his evil was spelled out as following the "way of Jeroboam" (16:25-26). Ahab is condemned in the same words (16:30), but his evil is spelled out at greater length (16:31-33a), and the initial condemnation is repeated in different and more vivid language: "Ahab did more to provoke the anger of the LORD, the God of Israel, than had all the kings of Israel who were before him" (16:33b). Ahab's "evil" comprises a list of several distinct crimes. First, like Omri, he continued to support the "sins of Jeroboam" (16:31a). Second, he married Jezebel, a Sidonian princess. Third, he worshiped the god Baal. Fourth, he promoted the cult of Baal by building a sanctuary to him in the capital city. Fifth, he "made a sacred pole," which implies involvement with the cult of the goddess Asherah as well.[9] Each of these indictments contributes to the image of Ahab. Jeroboam's

[9] Literally "he made the asherah." "Asherah" was the name of a goddess and was also used to refer to a wooden cult object that figured in her worship. Since the Hebrew has "*the* asherah" and speaks of Ahab "making" it, we should assume that the meaning here is the wooden cult object (the *NRSV*'s "sacred pole").

cult of the golden calves was condemned by Yahweh from its inception (1 Kgs 13:1-10). Marriage to a foreign woman was a violation of Deuteronomic law (Deut 7:1-5), and the dire consequences of such marriage were clearly manifest in Solomon's religious infidelity in his old age (1 Kgs 11:1-8), for which YHWH had decreed the political separation of the northern tribes from the Davidic kingdom of Judah. The connection between marriage to Jezebel and the following accusations of idolatry is already implied in the names of Jezebel and her father. "Ethbaal" (more properly "Ittobaal") was the king of Sidon in Phoenicia; his name means "Baal exists!" or perhaps "Baal is present!"—the first (even if camouflaged) occurrence of Baal's name in the book of Kings. And Jezebel's own name is compounded with the element -*zbl*, "Prince," a title applied frequently to Baal in Canaanite mythological texts.[10] The narrator portrays for us a king whose every deed (so far, at least) stands in direct violation of the Yahwistic values on which Israel is founded. And he does so in a way that subtly invites our assent. Note the unusual phrasing of v. 31: "And as if it had been a light thing for him to walk in the sins of Jeroboam son of Nebat, he took as his wife . . . ." To this point "to walk in the sins of Jeroboam" has been the ultimate evil of the Israelite kings (cf. 16:26). If Ahab considers it a "light thing," how can we not stand in horror of his utter depravity?[11]

The one event the narrator singles out from Ahab's reign is the rebuilding of the city of Jericho by Hiel of Bethel (16:34). Oddly, Ahab is not mentioned in the verse and we can only speculate whether there is anything to be learned about Ahab here and, if so, what it might be.[12] We know nothing of Hiel otherwise, though his origins as a Bethelite could evoke associations with the "sins of Jeroboam," whose calf cult was centered in Bethel. On the other hand, Jericho was a lush oasis in the desert of the Jordan valley (so lush, in fact, that much later in Roman times Cleopatra inveigled it as a gift from a besotted Marc Antony). It is unlikely that

---

[10] Compare the name Baalzebul, "Prince Baal," deformed into Baalzebub, "Lord of Flies," and used pejoratively in the New Testament for the "prince of devils." Jezebel's name, which probably meant something like "Where is the Prince?" *(i-zebul),* has been similarly deformed to *i-zebel,* "Where is the dung?" For further discussion of Jezebel's name, including the possibility that its original meaning may have been "The Prince Exists," see N. Avigad, "The Seal of Jezebel," *Israel Exploration Journal* 14 (1964) 274–76.

[11] In fact, the narrator's manipulation of our response is even stronger in the Hebrew text, where we are addressed with broken syntax and a direct question: "And then—was it a light thing that he walked in the sins of Jeroboam, son of Nebat?—he took as his wife . . . ."

[12] A good principle to employ in doing narrative criticism is that *everything* has an effect on a sensitive reader. A narrative without v. 34 would be slightly, but still sensibly, different from a narrative that contains it. The narrative critic's task is to identify and appreciate the potential effect on the sensitive reader of all components of the narrative.

anything so major as the rebuilding of a city there could have occurred without royal permission, if not royal patronage. To the knowledgeable reader, however, rebuilding Jericho reveals utter disdain for the will of YHWH: When Joshua destroyed Jericho during the Israelite conquest of the Promised Land he laid its reconstruction under a curse:

> Cursed before the LORD be anyone who tries to build this city—this Jericho!
> At the cost of his firstborn he shall lay its foundation,
> and at the cost of his youngest he shall set up its gates! (Josh 6:26)

Hiel's project demonstrates the potency of Joshua's curse,[13] but it simultaneously demonstrates the dismissive attitude toward YHWH prevalent in Ahab's day and, presumably, under his aegis.

At the end of this introductory material we have an unrelievedly negative image of Ahab. Everything the narrator has told us portrays a man actively in opposition to YHWH. Worse, he is the one who introduces into Israel the cult of YHWH's chief rival, Baal, as well as worship of the goddess Asherah.[14] Since these are our first impressions of Ahab, and they come to us from a presumably reliable narrator, they set the controlling context for our subsequent encounters with the king in the narrative world.

---

[13] It is not clear exactly what the text means in either passage by "at the cost of." It may imply no more than that the sons' deaths occurred accidentally in the course of construction. On the other hand, child sacrifice was not unknown in the ancient world (see, for instance, 2 Kings 3:21-27), including child sacrifice to assure the success and endurance of a construction. Children's bones, for instance, are sometimes found in the cornerstones of a building or a city wall.

[14] Historically the worship of Baal had long been indigenous to Israel. The cult of YHWH seems to have been the more recent development in the land. For this reason scholars have often tried to reconcile the biblical text with the data of history by suggesting that the Baal cult introduced by Ahab was that of Baal Melqart, Jezebel's Sidonian god, for whom her father Ittobaal was named. To the extent that the narrative may serve historical reconstruction, that is not impossible. As a reading of the *narrative,* however, it is unconvincing. In this narrative world no distinction is made between one form of Baal worship and another; and the absence of the god Baal from the biblical text since Judges 6:25-32, where Gideon destroyed his father's altar to Baal (who is apparently numbered among the "gods of the Amorites," 6:10) and its *asherah,* implies that his cult had been eradicated until Ahab reintroduced it. Certainly the text's collocation of "Jezebel, daughter of Ethbaal" with Ahab's Baalist innovations points to a connection between them: Ahab introduces the cult of Baal under Jezebel's influence. But in the narrative world (as distinct from what we believe we know about ancient Israelite history), this is not a mere matter of indulging his foreign wife with a chapel for her personal variety of worship; it represents the welcoming of a rival deity into YHWH's land.

CHAPTER TWO

Ahab in the Elijah Stories: 1 Kings 17–19

The narrator's usual pattern would be to proceed immediately from the single event cited from the king's reign to the stereotyped concluding formula. Instead he inserts two large narrative blocks, chapters 17–19, a series of stories featuring Elijah the Tishbite, and chapters 20–22, a series of stories wherein Ahab himself figures as the main character. As has been mentioned, this deviation from the standard shape of regnal accounts alerts the reader to two things: the importance of the reign of Ahab in the comprehensive narrative of the Israelite kingdoms, and the significance of Elijah (and, as we shall see, a multitude of other prophets) in shaping the story of that particular reign. The narrator's choice to put the Elijah narratives before those that focus on Ahab is determined first by chronology. Chapters 20–22 transpire during three years (22:1) at the very end of Ahab's life: He dies in 22:37.[1] The three years of the drought (see 18:1) presumably occurred earlier in Ahab's twenty-two-year reign. But the ordering of the two narrative blocks has another effect on readers as well. It suggests that, in order to understand Ahab, we must first understand Elijah. Only in light of what we learn by following Elijah's adventures will we be able to evaluate Ahab as the narrator wishes us to.

---

[1] In the Hebrew text chapter 21 functions to supply the reader a glimpse of internal affairs during the three years of peace between the wars of chapter 20 and that of chapter 22. This ordering of materials also establishes approximate balance between the three chapters of Elijah stories and the three chapters of Ahab stories. The ancient Greek translation of the Hebrew Bible, known as the Septuagint (LXX), organizes the account of Ahab's reign topically rather than narratively. By reversing the order of chapters 20 and 21 (Hebrew), it gathers all the stories of Elijah into a single series, followed by two chapters about Ahab and the Aramean wars.

Ahab plays only a secondary role in the Elijah narratives. In fact, aside from 17:1 and 19:1 he appears only in chapter 18, and even there not in its most dramatic scene, the contest on Mount Carmel (18:21-40). In 17:1 he is accosted by Elijah the Tishbite, of whom we have not previously heard and of whom we know nothing except a name, a descriptive term, and his Gileadite provenance.[2] Ahab himself neither acts nor speaks, and anything we conclude about him we must infer indirectly from what Elijah says. But who is Elijah, and how far can we rely on what he says? We cannot assume, as we are prone to do, everything that our familiarity with the biblical tradition tells us about Elijah the prophet. The narratee is hearing this story from the narrator for the first time and, to the extent we can, we ought to try to experience the linear unfolding of the narrative on the same terms. What do we know of Elijah at this point? The narrator does not call him "prophet" or anything of the sort. Elijah himself claims that he "stands before" YHWH, the God of Israel, which is idiomatic for standing in attendance upon someone as a servant would. Further, he claims personal authority over the rain: "There shall be neither dew nor rain these years, *except by my word.*" The implication, of course, is that this claim is somehow an instance of the service he performs for YHWH. But there is nothing in 17:1 to verify or falsify Elijah's claims, whether of servanthood or of power. In fact, the question of Elijah's reliability will be one of the important threads unifying chapter 17, culminating in the woman's profession in 17:24 that Elijah is "a man of God" and that the word in his mouth is truly YHWH's.[3] At that point the narrator will have shown us enough to establish Elijah's credentials, both as one who obeys YHWH (17:3-5, 9-10) and as one who speaks a word of power (17:16, 21-22); and the inferences about Ahab we can draw from 17:1 will be vindicated.

But what inferences can we draw from Elijah's challenge? By his claim to be a servant of YHWH, Elijah puts his confrontation with Ahab on a religious footing. This is entirely in keeping with what we have learned

---

[2] And even this information is uncertain. The standard English rendering, "Elijah the Tishbite of Tishbe in Gilead," conceals a problematic text. Ancient Hebrew did not write vowels; native speakers would have known how to pronounce the text without them. Elijah is identified as a "Tishbite" (*tšby,* pronounced "tishbiy"), but the term "Tishbite" is otherwise unknown. In form it usually indicates a place of origin (compare "Israel*ite,*" "Moab*ite,*" etc.). The text goes on to say that Elijah was from *tšby* in Gilead. The ancient Greek translators read this as indicating a place name and rendered it "Tishbe in Gilead," though we have no knowledge of such a location. The Hebrew tradition, however, pronounces the word "toshabey," meaning "the sojourners." This would indicate that Elijah was not native to Gilead (a region east of the Jordan settled by Israelites) but only a temporary resident there.

[3] Tracing this motif fully lies outside the scope of this book. See my *1 Kings* (Collegeville: Liturgical Press, 1996) 234–35.

about Ahab already, which emphasized religious issues, and particularly Ahab's patronage of the cult of Baal. But the fact that Elijah proclaims *drought* is itself pregnant with meaning. He is not simply imposing a punishment on Ahab and Israel for infidelity to YHWH. Baal's claim to divine power was his control of the weather, and in particular of the rain that is essential for the growth of crops in Israel, where rivers provide virtually no convenient water for agriculture and irrigation. Among Baal's titles in Canaanite mythology is "Rider on the Clouds," and he is often depicted wielding a thunderbolt.[4] For YHWH—or Elijah, claiming authority in YHWH's name—to assert control over the rain is to throw down the gauntlet to Baal himself. Behind the visible conflict of Elijah and Ahab looms the invisible rivalry of YHWH and Baal. And the figure of Ahab, then, is no longer merely that of a king whose support of things Baalist is "more evil than all who were before him," but that of one who represents Baal as Elijah represents YHWH.

Elijah versus Ahab stands surrogate for YHWH versus Baal. This heightened dimension forms the context for the role Ahab plays in chapter 18. YHWH has sent Elijah back to confront Ahab once again so that[5] the drought may be brought to an end (18:1). While Elijah journeys from Sidon, the narrator shifts to Samaria to show us a brief scene between Ahab and his majordomo, Obadiah (18:2b-6).[6] Three years of drought have resulted in crop failure; there is, therefore, famine as well as lack of drinking water. Ahab is about to send Obadiah out in a desperate search for fodder for the livestock, but the narrator interrupts the scene with a long, rambling digression that describes Obadiah, his devotion to YHWH, and the dangerous measures that devotion has led him to in thwarting the queen's pogrom. Stylistically the interruption is very odd. It is true that this is the

---

[4] Psalm 29, the majesty of God in the storm, is generally thought to be modeled on a Canaanite hymn to Baal. The "voice of the Lord," mentioned seven times in the poem, refers to thunder, and the lightning is mentioned in v. 7.

[5] There is a nuance in the Hebrew that the *NRSV*'s rendering ("I will send rain on the earth") misses. The Hebrew expresses purpose, as though Elijah's confrontation with Ahab were a necessary precondition for the return of rain: "Go, show yourself to Ahab *so that* I may send rain upon the earth."

[6] Obadiah is described as "over the house" (*NRSV*: "in charge of the palace"). Around a century earlier, in the days of Solomon, this office seems to have been a relatively minor internal and domestic one (1 Kgs 4:6); the holder was probably chief steward of the palace staff and royal estates. By the time of King Azariah of Judah, about one century after Ahab, the officer "over the house" had become second only to the king in the exercise of royal authority (see 2 Kgs 15:5 and Isa 22:15-24 [the *NRSV* translates the phrase as "master of the household" here]). It is difficult to determine precisely what Obadiah's responsibilities were, but the scene shows that care for the royal stables and livestock fell to him.

first appearance of Obadiah in the text, and thus the *location* of the interruption is perhaps explicable. But its length and detail are not. Obadiah
will never again appear in the Bible after 18:16; the reader should have no
need to know this much about him. Yet superfluous descriptive material is
virtually never found in Hebrew narrative. The ideal narratee will be alert
for a later payoff, and will not have long to wait.

Ahab's command to Obadiah (18:5) seems straightforward enough. It
is what one might expect of a conscientious monarch, and when in the next
verse Ahab himself personally pursues the search along with Obadiah we
may be inclined to admire him. Unfortunately, however, that is more the
result of a translator's oversight than of the narrator's manipulation. There
is an important verbal echo in the Hebrew that is lost in the *NRSV*. In describing Obadiah in v. 4 the narrator says he preserved YHWH prophets
"when Jezebel was killing off [literally, 'cutting off,' *hakrît,* from *krt,* 'to
cut']⁷ the prophets of the LORD." In v. 5 Ahab is concerned that he "not lose
[literally 'cut off,' *nakrît,* from the same verb] some of the animals." The
unusual metaphor, twice in close proximity, invites us to consider the statements together. We cannot be certain whether Ahab supported Jezebel's
persecution, but it is hardly likely that he was unaware of it. And so we see
a king who is concerned about "cutting off" animals but not about "cutting
off" human beings. The narrator's choice of words has transformed what
could be read as a testimony to royal conscientiousness into a subtle indicator of the king's perverted sense of values.

There is a further contrast in the passage, also to Ahab's disadvantage.
Ahab, the Baalist king, is desperately searching for watercourses that can
supply his livestock with fodder, but is unable to find any. Obadiah, the
faithful Yahwist (his very name, *'ōbad-yāhû,* means "Servant of YHWH"), is
able to supply his hundred hidden prophets with "bread *and water.*" There
is a foreshadowing here of the outcome of the tale: The servant of YHWH
will succeed where the servant of Baal will fail, because YHWH, not Baal,
controls the forces of nature. The contrast between Ahab and Obadiah is
aptly symbolized in v. 6: They are moving separately, and in opposite
directions.

---

⁷ The use of *krt* here is clearly significant. Comparison of the narrator's description of
Obadiah in vv. 3b-4 with Obadiah's self-description in vv. 12b-13 shows virtually verbatim
repetition. There are only two significant variations. Where the narrator described Obadiah
as revering YHWH "greatly," Obadiah describes himself as revering YHWH "from my youth."
The difference probably points up Obadiah's modesty: He sees his behavior as fidelity to
long-held values but not necessarily as something exceptional. The second variation is in this
verb. The narrator's use of *krt* in v. 4 points to the same verb in v. 5, whereas Obadiah's use
of *hrg* ("to kill") in v. 13 echoes his use of the same verb in vv. 12a and 14.

Obadiah's search leads him not to provender but to the prophet. Ahab does not appear in this scene (18:7-15), but he is the center of discussion. Elijah sends Obadiah to fetch Ahab, whom he calls Obadiah's "lord." The remark is not innocent. Elijah implies that Obadiah, who by name ("Servant of YHWH") as well as by deed appears to be a faithful Yahwist, is in the end nothing more than a servant of the Baalist king. Obadiah's response is frantic. He babbles, he repeats himself, he interrupts himself. His fear is evident, but its basis is only partly apparent. Obviously, if he comes to Ahab to announce the whereabouts of a prophet the king has been seeking for three years he will be suspected of having harbored Elijah all that time. It is not true, of course, but Obadiah *has* been hiding a hundred other prophets, and he certainly wants neither them nor himself to be discovered. However, there is more to Obadiah's fear, but it is hidden in the Hebrew. Elijah commands him to tell Ahab, "Elijah is here." In Hebrew that sentence is *hinnēh ʾēlîyāhû,* which is aurally indistinguishable from *hinnēh ʾēlî yāhû,* "Behold—YHWH is my God." In order to comply with Elijah's command Obadiah must reveal himself to Ahab as a worshiper of YHWH. He certainly risks his influential position as majordomo, and quite possibly his life. Amid his protests that Elijah's order amounts to a death sentence for him (vv. 9, 12, 14), Obadiah tells us two things about Ahab: First, that he has been searching for Elijah everywhere, presumably with no benevolent intent. He has even been applying diplomatic pressure on his international allies, "requiring an oath" that Elijah was not in their country. Second, if he is thwarted again in his desire to arrest Elijah he may become murderous.

Both statements contribute to the characterization of Ahab, but before we explore them we must ask a prior question: Can we believe Obadiah? Even if he is basically devout and honest, he has been living a double life; he is therefore capable of dissimulation. He is, moreover, seriously panicked and may be indulging in rhetorical exaggeration. However, the narrator gives us a clear indication that Obadiah's words are true and accurate. In the course of his speech Obadiah repeats information we have already learned from the reliable narrator (compare 18:12b-13 with 18:3b-4). The repetition is almost verbatim and the few differences are explicable in ways that cast no doubt on Obadiah's veracity (see n. 7 above). Obadiah is therefore reliable, and we can trust what he says about Ahab.

The first thing Obadiah tells us about Ahab shows us how intensely the king has sought the prophet. Obadiah's fear that announcing Elijah's presence will be dangerous suggests that Ahab's desire to find Elijah is based on anger rather than on repentance or hope. But hidden in this brief dramatic sketch is a stroke of bitter satire. Elijah has been in "Zarephath, which belongs to Sidon" (17:8). Surely one of the international allies Ahab would have consulted is Ethbaal, king of Sidon, Ahab's own father-in-law (16:31). Baal and his supporters cannot find the YHWH prophet even when he is in their own territory! Obadiah's second revelation juxtaposes Ahab's likely killing (Hebrew *hrg*) of Obadiah with Jezebel's killing (Hebrew *hrg;* see n. 7 above) of YHWH's prophets. This implies, without explicitly saying it, that Ahab's attitude toward those who support Yahwism is not that different from Jezebel's. It is not clear whether that represents long-standing royal policy or rather a recent favoring of the cult of Baal in view of the three-year drought. The scene ends with Obadiah carrying Elijah's message, and presumably therefore renouncing his Baalist allegiances publicly. What becomes of him we are never told.

In the next scene Ahab and Elijah come face to face. Ahab's first words to Elijah are a scathing challenge, but their precise meaning is ambivalent. Ahab's accusation that Elijah "troubles" Israel could be understood to mean that he recognizes Elijah's—and therefore YHWH's—power over the rain, and blames Elijah for causing the drought. This would mean that his attachment to Baal is in some measure hypocritical: He knows YHWH is more powerful, yet for some reason obstinately resists worshiping him. It is more likely, however, that Ahab sincerely acknowledges Baal's control of the rain and feels that the drought is Baal's punishment on Israel for Elijah's insult to Baal. Elijah has not *caused* the drought, but his arrogance in asserting YHWH's control over the rain occasioned this demonstration of Baal's power. This attitude would be more consistent with what we know of Ahab to this point. Elijah's response turns the indictment back on Ahab. He accuses the whole family of Omri ("you . . . and your father's house . . . have forsaken")[8] of spurning "the commandments of the LORD"—in other words, of following the "sins of Jeroboam." Ahab himself has gone egregiously further and "followed the Baals." And so Elijah confirms in different words the judgments of the narrator in 16:25-26 and 30-33.

Elijah continues with a command to Ahab.[9] The Elijah narrative includes a number of command-and-compliance exchanges (e.g., 17:2-6,

---

[8] Hebrew, unlike English, distinguishes singular and plural "you." In 18:18 all the second-person forms are singular, referring to Ahab, except "you have forsaken," which is plural and encompasses "you and your father's house." The *NRSV*'s translation is misleading. By rendering "you have forsaken . . . and followed" it gives the impression that the subject of the two verbs is the same. But the first verb is plural and the second is singular. "You and your father's house" have forsaken . . . but only "you [i.e., Ahab] have followed . . . ."

[9] Elijah's boldness in issuing a command to the king is not untypical of him. Already in chapter 17 he challenged YHWH's justice and petitioned him for redress (17:20-21). YHWH did exactly what Elijah asked (17:22b). The narrator even tells us that "The LORD *listened to the voice of* Elijah" (17:22a)—the standard Hebrew idiom for "obeyed"!

8-10, 13-16, 20-22; 18:1-2a). In many cases the account of the compliance implies the exact match of command and fulfillment, either by repeating the wording of the command almost verbatim or by saying in so many words that "X did according to the word of Y." Here, however, Ahab's compliance with Elijah's command, while generally in conformity with it, leaves the exactitude of Ahab's behavior in doubt. He does not "assemble Israel with the prophets," he "assembles the prophets." And it is not clear that he assembles *all* the prophets: Elijah demanded "the 450 prophets of Baal and the 400 prophets of Asherah"; Ahab assembles "the prophets," with no further specification. Indeed, the prophets of Asherah are never again mentioned in the story. The effect is to signal the king's obedience to the prophet's command, but to suggest at the same time that the obedience may have been grudging and imperfect.

Strangely, Ahab disappears from the story at this point and is completely absent from the narrative of the contest on Mount Carmel. Narratively his role is filled by the prophets of Baal, who stand in opposition to Elijah as representatives of their god (just as the people of Israel are the narrative continuation of the ambivalent Obadiah's role). But the only thing to note about Ahab as a character is his absence. He is not absent from the entire event, however: In 18:41, after Elijah has slaughtered the prophets of Baal at the Wadi Kishon, he tells Ahab to climb Mount Carmel himself. We are apparently to assume that, for some reason, Ahab remained at the bottom of Mount Carmel during the contest. What could this signify? There are two keys to unlocking this question: First, the whole Elijah story contains a series of allusions to the adventures of Moses and the Israelites in the desert after the Exodus; second, "down" and "up"—particularly "up" on top of a mountain—have metaphorical value in the Elijah story. The Moses allusions generally focus on Elijah himself,[10] but secondary aspects of that motif touch others in the story as well. Here Ahab has the position of the people of Israel at Sinai. Moses ascends the mountain to meet YHWH, but the people remain at the mountain's foot. It may seem strange to parallel Ahab's role here with that of the people in Exodus while the people themselves are on the top of Carmel. But the Elijah narrative and the contest itself are not primarily about the allegiance of the people. The people, in their own imperfect way, have not abandoned YHWH; they have tried to *combine* the worship of YHWH with that of Baal (see 18:21). Ahab, on the other hand, has entirely broken covenant with YHWH by apparently exclusive adherence to Baal (18:18). The people's allegiance is important, but the king's acceptance of the demands of the Sinai

---

[10] For a fuller discussion of this topic see my *1 Kings,* 284–89.

covenant is paramount. Like Israel at Sinai, he must remain at the foot of the mountain until the covenant is made. This also points to the second key, the contrast of "down," the sphere of everyday life, and "up," the locus of divine encounter. In chapter 17 Elijah takes the woman's son *up* to his chamber to confront Yhwh and ask for the boy's resuscitation; he brings the boy back *down* to return him alive to his mother. Here in chapter 18 both the miracle of fire and, as we shall see, the miracle of rain occur on the mountaintop. Each is followed by a descent and return to the mundane world: the slaughter of the Baal prophets and the hurried ride to Jezreel. In chapter 19 Elijah will once again climb a mountain, this time Horeb itself, to meet God, and come down again to enmesh himself in worldly political affairs. At the foot of Carmel, Ahab must await Yhwh's victory over Baal before the mediator can offer him the chance to renew the covenant.

This invitation comes in the final scene of the chapter. The prophets of Baal are dead, Ahab is back on stage. Elijah commands him to "Go up, eat, and drink," and justifies his command with the promise of the return of rain. Why can Ahab not refresh himself where he is instead of climbing the mountain to do so? It is another allusion to the Moses-Sinai traditions. After the overwhelming theophany of Yhwh at Sinai and the giving of the covenant law (Exodus 19–23), Yhwh invites Moses, Aaron and two of his sons, and seventy elders of Israel to the top of the mountain, though only Moses will approach Yhwh himself (24:1-2). To prepare for the event, the people ratify the covenant (24:3-8). Those invited then climb the mountain, where they "beheld God, and they ate and drank" (24:9-11). The meal at the top of the mountain is a meal of theophany and covenant-making. Elijah invites Ahab to "go up [where he will experience the theophany of the return of rain], eat and drink [i.e., seal the covenant with a meal in Yhwh's presence]."

This brief element in the story—Ahab's position at the foot of the mountain and Elijah's invitation to him to climb the mountain for a covenant meal—adds a surprising new facet to the figure of Ahab. Yhwh is willing to restore his covenantal relationship with this Baalist king. While this tells us much about Yhwh's forbearance, about Ahab it reveals only a new possibility. But it is a possibility we have had no previous glimpse of: Ahab may, if he chooses, return to Yhwh and restore the fortunes of Israel. Does he so choose? The narrator subtly, but powerfully, refuses to say. Elsewhere, in order to indicate perfect obedience, the narrator will repeat the words of the command in the compliance. Here he modifies the verb forms to infinitives; he does not say, "Ahab went up, ate, and drank," but "Ahab went up *to eat and to drink*." Ahab has been invited to renounce his Baalist ways and renew the covenant with Yhwh, but the narrator leaves us in suspense about his response. When all is said and done we still do not know whether he in fact ate and drank the covenant meal or not. Ahab's headlong rush to Jezreel to outpace the storm is similarly ambiguous: Is it the triumphant procession of a renewed monarch, heralded by his prophet, or is it the flight of a recalcitrant king before the power of a deity he refuses to serve?

The suspense endures throughout chapter 19. The only mention of Ahab in the entire chapter is 19:1, where we are told that Ahab reported the events of chapter 18 to Jezebel.[11] Ahab's readiness to inform Jezebel that Elijah has slaughtered her favorites is not encouraging, but since the narrator merely reports the matter to us and does not give us scene and dialogue we cannot be sure. It is not impossible to imagine that Ahab's message aimed to point out to Jezebel the futility of trying to stand against YHWH. The remainder of the chapter focuses on Elijah's response to Jezebel's threat, and the theophany he experiences at Horeb. Ahab does not appear again in the chapter, nor does he figure in Elijah's dialogue with YHWH. (Elijah blames his straits on "the Israelites," not on Ahab.) One element foreshadows later developments in the characterization of Ahab; that is YHWH's speech in 19:15-18. From it we learn two things. The first is that Israel's political future will entail bloody disaster for the ruling house emanating from without—Hazael of Damascus—and from within—Jehu's coup d'état. Although neither Hazael nor Jehu will come to power until after the reign of Ahab, the two figures foreshadow the stories of Ahab in 1 Kings 20–22. In 1 Kings 20 and 22, Damascus (under Ben-hadad, Hazael's predecessor) will be Israel's enemy and Ahab's bane, and in 1 Kings 21 Ahab will instigate the judicial murder of Naboth that Jehu later cites to justify his *lèse majesté* (2 Kgs 9:25-26). The second thing we learn from YHWH's speech is that his decrees remain rooted in his rivalry with Baal.

And so, at the end of the block of narratives that feature Elijah, our picture of Ahab has grown more nuanced, but not significantly different. He is an unrelievedly Baalist king, with no apparent concern for YHWH or for the protection of YHWH's cult. YHWH has unexpectedly offered him a covenant relationship, but his response still hangs in suspense. And YHWH's hostility to Baal and his minions is absolute.

---

[11] The Hebrew text here is suspect, though the meaning is clear. Literally the Hebrew reads: "Ahab told Jezebel all that Elijah had done and all that he had killed all the prophets with the sword." It seems likely that, somewhere along the line, an inattentive scribe accidentally miscopied his text.

CHAPTER THREE

Ahab in the Ahab Stories: 1 Kings 20–22

Narrative Criticism 2

Before we turn to the stories that feature Ahab himself as the central figure (1 Kings 20–22) we must pause to take a closer look at an element of biblical narrative we have so far considered only briefly: the narrator. To this point our encounters with the narrator have been relatively straightforward. The narrator has given us a coherent, if relentlessly dark, character sketch of Ahab, with the only glimmer of light an uncertain hope: YHWH offered Ahab the opportunity to renew his covenantal relationship; whether Ahab did so or not remains unsaid. From this point on, however, as Ahab moves center stage, the narrator's presentation of him will become more complex and we will need more refined theoretical tools to deal with it.

The essential principle whose implications we must explore has been mentioned already. The narrator is *not* the author (see above, Chapter One). This is most clearly seen when a story is narrated by one of the characters involved. Herman Melville's *Moby Dick* begins with the words, "Call me Ishmael"; we know, then, that the voice telling us the story belongs to a sailor on the *Pequod,* and not to Melville. The same is less obvious but no less true of transparent third-person narrators (which is the situation in most passages of the Hebrew Bible). The voice that tells us that "King Ben-hadad of Aram gathered all his army together" (1 Kgs 20:1) belongs to an unnamed *narrator,* and not—or not immediately, at least—to the flesh-and-blood human being who first penned the words.

Our inveterate temptation to collapse author and narrator into a single being is understandable, but it depends on our ignoring the uniqueness of written storytelling. We tend to conceptualize a written story in the simpler terms of oral storytelling: A storyteller communicates a tale to his or her audience. Our model is, perhaps, a tribal elder passing lore on to the young, or a parent telling stories of early married life to an adult son or daughter, or a camp counselor entertaining the youngsters around a campfire. In a written story, however, there is an intermediary not present in the oral setting: the *text*. The author creates a text, the reader reads the text. A reader's experience of receiving the story comes not from direct encounter with an author but through the voice that "utters" the text in the reader's (metaphorical) hearing. That voice is the narrator's.

Recognizing the distance between this intermediate "voice" and the author opens up several significant implications. First, the narrator need not have the same characteristics as the author. Although it is not often an issue in the biblical text, where narrators are usually transparent, a male Israelite author could in theory create a female narrator (and vice versa), or a non-Israelite narrator, or even a non-human one. More importantly, an author can create a narrator with whom the author *disagrees*. This is clearly the case in some modern literature, where the narrator is lying or insane. But without going to such extremes one can certainly envisage a case where an author, for whatever purpose, might construct a narrator whose tale promotes a point of view slightly askew from the author's own.

This possibility is more clearly seen, perhaps, if we think about another potential difference between narrator and author. The author is a singular person[1]—but the narrator need not be. Let's return to one of our models of oral storytelling: a parent telling stories of early married life to an adult son or daughter. Put *both* parents in the picture. Now *two* narrative voices, sometimes in unison, sometimes in harmony, occasionally in discord, weave a braided tale. There is no reason an author could not construct a narrative along such lines, with two (or more!) narrative voices each making its unique contribution to the story. In such a model it is clear that the

---

[1] This statement conceals a whole dimension of theoretical complexity. Biblical texts in their canonical form are, in most cases, composite products of whole series of oral tradents, writers, editors, and even occasionally translators. Their authors are rarely if ever "singular persons." The singular "author" of whom I speak above is, in the technical jargon of literary critics, the "implied author." That term refers to the *assumption* a reader must make if he or she is to read a text as a coherent, meaningful literary unity: To do so, the reader must posit a unitary mind and intention behind the text. This "author," who exists only to the degree that a coherent, singular reading of the text *implies* such an existence, is, in the last analysis, a *construct by the reader* out of ideological clues found in the text. Under normal circumstances the "implied author," unlike the narrator, ought to manifest something of the viewpoint and intention of the flesh-and-blood person(s) who created the text (though of course an implied author will never incorporate more than a subset of a real author's personality). "Implied author" is therefore a useful analytical category: It establishes a *pied-à-terre,* so to speak, for an authorial presence and intention within the text.

author's point of view cannot be simply equated with any one of the narrative voices', any more than the author's point of view can be equated with that of one of the named characters in the story. The author's point of view is communicated by the *whole* narrative and all the voices that constitute it.

This places a heavy responsibility on the reader. He or she cannot simply take one of the voices in the text as articulating the author's "message." No single character—not even the narrator—is the exclusive "mouthpiece" of the author. The reader must infer the authorial viewpoint from all the clues and all the voices, both characters' and narrators', that form the fabric of the narrative. This will be our task as we listen to the conflicting narrative voices that tell us the stories of Ahab and the Aramean wars.

King Ahab—the Ahab Stories

The stories of King Ahab in 1 Kings 20–22 fall into two categories. Chapters 20 and 22 tell of wars between King Ahab and King Ben-hadad of Aram (or Damascus);[2] chapter 21 tells of some internal affairs in Ahab's kingdom during the three-year lull between the wars of chapters 20 and 22. Although the portrayals of Ahab in the two chapters of war stories are similar not only in their subject matter but also in their narrative strategy, the reader will not encounter them together in succession. The events that intervene in chapter 21 will have a decisive impact on the way a reader perceives the Ahab of chapter 22. And so we will consider the three chapters in their linear, canonical order[3] and take note of the common features of chapters 20 and 22 only after we have looked at all three chapters.

Chapter 20: Ahab and the Aramean Wars: Ahab's Victories

Chapter 20 tells the story of Ahab's military resistance to two invasions by Ben-hadad of Aram and the unexpected victory YHWH gives Ahab. The first part of the chapter is symmetrically arranged in an ABB'A'

---

[2] Aram, the country, is sometimes referred to by the name of its capital city, Damascus. Its location approximates that of modern-day Syria, though Aram was rather smaller. (Sometimes translations will render "Aram" as "Syria.")

[3] That is, in their canonical order in the standard Hebrew text. It is noteworthy that, in the ancient Greek translation (the "Septuagint," translated in Alexandria, Egypt, in the third to second centuries B.C.E.), the material in chapters 20 and 21 (Hebrew) comes in reverse order. This produces a text with four chapters about Elijah (corresponding to Hebrew chapters 17–19, 21) followed by two chapters about Ahab's Aramean wars (corresponding to Hebrew chapters 20 and 22). Such a substantial rearrangement of material makes the Greek text potentially quite different as a narrative. Since our concern in this book is with the standard Hebrew text, we will not detour to explore those differences.

pattern. It begins with three exchanges of diplomatic messages between Ben-hadad and Ahab (20:1-12) followed by an account of the battle of Samaria (20:13-21). A year later a further campaign occurs, with a battle at Aphek (20:22-30). In the aftermath of Ahab's decisive victory, three exchanges of diplomatic messages between Ben-hadad and Ahab ensue to finalize a treaty that recognizes the new state of affairs and establishes peace (20:31-34).[4] The last verses of the chapter (20:35-43) fall outside the pattern and introduce a surprising twist: In YHWH's name a prophet condemns Ahab for the treaty he made.

20:1-34

The opening series of diplomatic negotiations portrays Ben-hadad of Aram and Ahab of Israel as foils for one another. Ben-hadad is powerful, arrogant, high-handed; Ahab is, at least to begin with, subservient, polite, compliant. Ben-hadad has invaded Israel with a superior army and besieged Ahab in his capital at Samaria. He demands Ahab's submission as a vassal. His messengers' opening words, "Thus says Ben-hadad," are an example of what is called the "messenger formula," used by envoys of a superior power to address messages to an inferior.[5] The text does not reveal whether Ben-hadad seeks to conquer Israel and impose vassalage upon Ahab or Ahab was already Ben-hadad's vassal and the latter is demanding a reaffirmation of that status. In either case Ahab capitulates, professes fealty to Ben-hadad as his overlord (note the title with which he addresses Ben-hadad in 20:4, "my lord, O king"), and makes the required formal declaration of vassalage that all he possesses belongs to his suzerain. In this first exchange there is no indication of Ahab's motivation—is he cowardly? is he merely being prudent?—nor does the narrator imply any clear evaluation of his behavior. About all we can say is that he is polite.

In the second exchange Ben-hadad betrays his real agenda. He misrepresents his earlier message, claiming that his demand for a formal declara-

---

[4] A reverse symmetrical pattern like ABB'A' often reflects a contrast in contents. Here we have Ben-hadad's arrogant bluster (subunit A) contrasted with his groveling (subunit A'). The two battle scenes, on the other hand, display intensification rather than contrast. In the battle of Samaria a small (seven thousand: 20:15) Israelite force inflicts a "great slaughter" (20:21) on superior Aramean troops. In the battle of Aphek a tiny Israelite force ("like two little flocks of goats," 20:27) miraculously wipes out an enormous Aramean army. On the interpretive dynamics of symmetrical structures see Jerome T. Walsh, *Style and Structure in Biblical Hebrew Narrative* (Collegeville: Liturgical Press, 2001).

[5] The formula is originally a secular one—see, for example 2 Kings 18:19—but it is regularly used by Israelite prophets to deliver God's word as well.

tion had been a demand for *delivery.* Such tribute of goods and persons (the royal family would be held as hostages) would normally have been required only of a vassal who had rebelled and been defeated. In the story we have, this is not the case. Not only is any account of such a rebellion lacking; if Ahab had been guilty of rebellion, Ben-hadad would surely have adverted to it as grounds for his demands. Everything points to the conclusion that Ben-hadad is not negotiating in good faith. He seeks plunder, whether by voluntary concession or violent conquest. His threat is particularly provocative; his plunderers, says Ben-hadad, will take away everything Ahab prizes.[6] Ahab does not immediately reply to this escalation of hostilities. The reader, however, cannot help but feel sympathy for him: Ben-hadad is acting the bully, and Ahab, despite his deference, is defenseless.

Before he responds to the Aramean, Ahab turns to "all the elders of the land"—that is, the leading citizens of the towns and villages outside the capital city. Accustomed as we are to the values and practices of democracy, this impresses us far less than it should. In an absolute monarchy, kings had their advisors, but they were neither required nor expected to consult the citizenry.[7] That Ahab does so reflects an awareness that, should he refuse to capitulate, not only will he and his capital suffer, but also the surrounding countryside and, perhaps, the entire kingdom could be devastated. There is another subtle touch that speaks well of Ahab. Where Ben-hadad demanded "your silver and gold . . . your fairest wives and children," suggesting that tribute had priority over hostages, Ahab says that Ben-hadad demanded "my wives, my children, my silver, and my gold," suggesting that for Ahab his family's danger causes greater anxiety than the loss of wealth. This whole speech presents Ahab, then, as concerned about his citizens and their well-being, aware of the broad responsibility he holds for them, and admirably valuing people above things. His willingness to consult the elders also suggests that, should they advise him to capitulate, he is willing to undergo personal deprivation of family and wealth in order to spare his country from the depredations of war. The elders'[8]

---

[6] The *NRSV,* following the ancient translations, says that Ben-hadad's servants shall "lay hands on whatever pleases *them,*" but the Hebrew text actually reads "on whatever pleases *you.*"

[7] In fact, in some cultures, to do so would be considered a royal dereliction of duty and an attempt to evade responsibility; there is no evidence in the text, however, of such a negative judgment on Ahab's action.

[8] The narrator associates "all the people" with "all the elders" in this reply. This may imply that the elders' sentiments were widely echoed throughout the populace. However, the use of the phrase "all the people" elsewhere to mean specifically the army (see, for instance, 20:15) does not allow us to draw this conclusion with confidence.

reply is revealing. They tell him, "Do not listen or consent."[9] The implication is clear: The elders, representing the people, are willing to stand with
Ahab in their resistance to Ben-hadad's extortion. Ahab is trusted by his
people.

Although his resistance is now stiffened by popular support, Ahab remains polite and submissive, even in his rejection of the Aramean demands. He continues to address Ben-hadad as "my lord the king," and he
couches his response in the less challenging terms of an inability ("I cannot") than of a refusal ("I will not").

Ben-hadad's reaction to Ahab's refusal is a dire threat, emphasized by
an oath, that his army will obliterate the Israelite capital city. The gloves
are off, so to speak. And Ahab replies in kind, with a brilliantly laconic
proverb whose pithy punch cannot be preserved in translation. Literally he
says, "Let one who buckles on not boast like one who unbelts" (the
proverb is only four words in Hebrew!). Given the military context of the
scene, the *NRSV*'s reading of the proverb as having to do with putting on
armor and taking it off is not inappropriate. But literally the proverb refers
to strapping on some item of apparel and unbuckling something from
around the waist. Independent of the present context, it probably refers to
dressing in the morning and undressing at night, and warns against boasting of the day's accomplishments before one has actually accomplished
them. In other words, "Don't count your chickens before they've hatched."
Ahab's words are defiant (he no longer calls Ben-hadad "my lord the
king"), courageous, and clever.

On the whole, this first subunit of the story presents us with an Ahab
very different indeed from what we might have expected. Gone is the unrelievedly negative picture of a Baalist king. In its place we have a compli-
mentary portrayal of a king caught in a diplomatic dilemma, respectful of
and admired by his people, who balances deference and defiance toward
his overlord deftly and courageously.

This positive depiction of Ahab continues in the next subunit of the
story, the battle of Samaria (20:13-21). Preparations for the battle are described at some length and comprise two parts: a dialogue between an
anonymous prophet of YHWH and King Ahab, and a narrative that describes the engagement itself. In view of what we have seen of Ahab in earlier chapters, the prophet's address to the king is startling. He delivers a
positive message from YHWH, a promise of victory. YHWH even deigns to

---

[9] The Hebrew wording makes the second command a bit stronger than the first; this is
not reflected in the *NRSV*. In order to capture this nuance one could render: "Do not listen;
above all, do not consent!"

design military tactics for him (20:14: "Thus says the LORD"), specifying the order in which Israelite troops should engage the enemy: first the "young men who serve the district governors,"[10] then the army, and finally Ahab himself.[11] The narrative that follows recounts how those divine instructions were meticulously carried out and victory ensued.

Ahab shows no surprise at YHWH's favor. On the contrary, his response is immediate and open. His questions are not challenges to the prophet's message; rather, they express Ahab's desire for the details of what YHWH would have him do. Once he has received his instructions, he carries them out to the letter: The "young men who serve the district governors" sortie from Samaria first (20:17), then the rest of the army (20:19), and finally Ahab (20:21). Ahab clearly has YHWH's favor, and his prompt and careful obedience suggests that he, for his part, is duly devoted to YHWH.

After the battle has been won, YHWH's favor continues. "The" prophet (therefore, presumably the same prophet as before in 20:13) forewarns Ahab that the next spring will see another Aramean attack (20:22; the battle account follows in 20:23-30). And so it happens. The Arameans engage the Israelites at Aphek the next spring and are again defeated. King Ahab appears only twice in the subunit, both times as the recipient of favorable prophetic messages from YHWH (20:22, 28). Nothing is said of his words or deeds.

---

[10] The meaning of the phrase "young men who serve the district governors" is disputed. Many scholars see them as some sort of specialized shock troops or commandos. The Hebrew word *na'ar* ("young man"), however, can carry connotations of being in service for training, something like "cadet" or "recruit." For that reason some have recently proposed that the "young men who serve the district governors" who lead the Israelite attack are untrained adolescents and their "service" may be civil, not military. Militarily they would be, in effect, raw recruits. This interpretation comports well with the pattern seen in Judges 7:1-8 and 1 Samuel 17:31-49, where the combatants' lack of experience and training demonstrates clearly the decisive presence of YHWH in the battle. See the remarks in Mordechai Cogan, *I Kings: A New Translation with Introduction and Commentary*, AB 10 (New York: Doubleday, 2000) 464–65; Iain W. Provan, *1 and 2 Kings*, New International Biblical Commentary on the Old Testament (Peabody, MA: Hendrickson, 1995) 155; and Brandon L. Fredenburg, *With Horns of Irony: The Implications of Irony in the Account of Ahab's Reign (1 Kings 16:29–22:40)*, Ph.D. Dissertation, The Iliff School of Theology and The University of Denver (Colorado Seminary), 2003 (Ann Arbor: University Microfilms, 2004) 180–81, n. 146. As Fredenburg points out, the ancient Greek version, the Septuagint, seems to have understood the phrase this way, translating the Hebrew *nĕʿārîm* with the Greek *ta paidaria*, "small boys."

[11] There is an uncertainty in the Hebrew here. In 20:14b Ahab asks, literally, "Who shall bind the battle?" The meaning of the idiom is unsure. The *NRSV* takes it as meaning "to initiate battle" (compare the English "to join battle"); others take it as meaning "to finish the battle" (compare the English "to wrap things up"). The only other appearance of the idiom in the Hebrew Bible is 2 Chronicles 13:3, where it does not seem any more specific than "to engage in battle." Given the battle order as it unfolds (20:15-21), with Ahab entering battle last, it seems here to mean "to wrap up the battle."

Nevertheless, several inferences about him can be drawn from other details in the narrative. First, the battle takes place not at Samaria but at Aphek. The location of Aphek is debated. It was, presumably, on level ground in accord with the Aramean strategy of 20:25. In the opinion of many scholars, the most likely site is on the Transjordanian plateau east of the south end of the Sea of Galilee, on the most direct road from Damascus to Israel. (There is in this region a spring known in Arabic as *al-Fīq*, which reflects the Hebrew "Aphek.") This Transjordanian territory was contested between Aram and Israel. Ahab's presence there suggests a readiness to defend borders, or even to extend his territory, that was entirely absent from his subservient attitudes at the beginning of the chapter. He has grown in strength and in assertiveness in favor of Israel.

Second, the several parallels between the two battle accounts urge us to read them comparatively. Each involves divine words promising victory to Ahab, and the words are strikingly similar (compare 20:13 with 20:28). Each contrasts the Aramean and Israelite camps (compare 20:15-18 with 20:27). Each describes the battle itself with utmost brevity (20:20aα: three words; and 20:29bβ: ten words). Each ends with a description of the separate flights of the Aramean survivors and of Ben-hadad (20:20aβ and 20:30). The several similarities serve to point up some significant differences. In the battle of Samaria, Ben-hadad's "army" (20:1) faces Ahab's seven thousand troops (20:15);[12] for the battle of Aphek, Ben-hadad musters "the Arameans" to fight against "Israel" (20:26). What began as hostility between one king's troops and another's has become hostility of one people against the other. No longer are the stakes the plunder of a capital city; they threaten the nation itself. Ahab's role is no longer that of rebellious vassal; he now stands for his whole people, and what he does he does *as Israel,* obedient to YHWH.[13]

Third, even YHWH recognizes Ahab's status as representative of the whole nation. In 20:13 the prophet promised Ahab victory so that "*you* shall know that I am the LORD." This "you" is singular, directed personally

---

[12] The text speaks of "all the people, all the sons of Israel" (*NRSV:* "all the people of Israel"). The number "seven thousand," however, makes it clear that the reference is not to the whole populace but to the troops. For the same idiomatic use of "all the people" to mean the army see 1 Kings 16:16: "And *the people* [*NRSV:* "troops"] who were encamped heard it said, 'Zimri has conspired, and he has killed the king'; therefore *all Israel* made Omri, the commander of the army, king over Israel that day in the camp" (emphasis added).

[13] For example, in 20:15 *Ahab* mustered the Israelite troops; in 20:27 the Israelite troops *are mustered.* The passive voice not only allows the mustering to be an Israelite action rather than merely a royal one; it is also an example of what Hebrew linguists call the "divine passive"—use of a passive verb to imply divine agency without stating it expressly.

to Ahab.[14] YHWH's word to Ahab in 20:28, however, still promises him the victory personally ("into *your* hand" is singular), but intends the victory so that "*you* [plural; that is, all the people] shall know that I am the LORD."[15]

In the account of the battle of Aphek, then, Ahab's character expands in stature despite his limited role in the prose. He remains favored of YHWH, but grows from admired leader of the people to representative—almost embodiment—of Israel and its nationhood. YHWH's support of Israel's efforts takes on almost mythological proportions—one hundred thousand foot soldiers killed in battle, another twenty-seven thousand crushed by the falling city wall (shades of Jericho!)—all so that *Ahab* may have victory and *Israel* may know that "I am YHWH."

After the battle of Aphek, as before the battle of Samaria, there are diplomatic negotiations between Ahab and Ben-hadad. In each case there are three exchanges of messages, but now the tables have been turned. Before Ahab's resounding victories over Aram, Ben-hadad was the power, imperious and domineering. Now, defeated, he is the suppliant, offering through his representatives to become Ahab's vassal (note "*your servant, Ben-hadad*," 20:32) in exchange for his life. Unlike Ben-hadad, Ahab exercises his power with dignity and magnanimity. He not only spares Ben-hadad's life; he treats him as an equal (note "He is *my brother*," 20:32b) and makes a treaty with him whose terms establish parity, not reversed vassalage, between the nations (20:34; contrast the terms of vassalage claimed by Ben-hadad in 20:2-3).

We learn much about Ahab in these negotiations, some of it by very subtle rhetorical and verbal clues slipped in by the narrator. Ben-hadad's advisors (*NRSV:* "servants," 20:31—presumably the same "servants" who advised him in 20:23) tell him of the Israelite kings' reputation for covenant loyalty, or *ḥesed* [*NRSV:* "merciful"].[16] They do so, however, with phrasing that resonates with overtones:

[14] In Hebrew, unlike English, the second person pronoun "you" has distinct forms for singular and plural, and for masculine and feminine. This affords clues to identify an addressee that are lost in translation.

[15] Even though it is not said in so many words, the victory is also, of course, so that *the Arameans* will know who YHWH is. It was, after all, their denigration of him as "a god of the hills" that led to this latest confrontation, as YHWH himself avers (20:28a).

[16] The term *ḥesed* is virtually impossible to translate accurately. It is essentially the inner commitment to a relationship that expresses not only devotion and loyalty to the partner (thus translations like "love," "faithfulness," "devotion," "loyalty"); it also conveys one's willingness to stand by the relationship even when the partner is unworthy (thus "mercy," "compassion," "kindness"). The term therefore often describes YHWH's commitment to the covenant with Israel as well as the response expected on Israel's part. It is not, however, restricted to the human relationship with God, but also forms part of any human covenant relationship.

We have heard . . .

kî malkê bêt yiśrā'el	that the kings of the house of Israel
kî malkê ḥesed hēm	indeed kings of *ḥesed* [are] they.

The strong parallelism of the Hebrew is clear from the repeated *kî malkê* (which is inevitably lost in translation because of the different syntactic functions of the word *kî*). It gives the saying a gnomic, almost poetic character, and emphasizes the identity of the two phrases, "kings of the house of Israel" and "kings of *ḥesed*." In the servants' view, to be a king of Israel *is* to be true to one's commitments (a subtle insinuation, perhaps, that to be a king of Aram is not?). And since Ahab had been Ben-hadad's vassal, the servants hold out hope that he may still be willing to show *ḥesed* to his former overlord. Of course, this opinion comes from advisors whose track record for accuracy is hardly impressive; these are the same ones who said that "their god is a mountain god" (20:23)![17] We cannot conclude, therefore, that Ahab *will* in fact show *ḥesed,* but we learn that the kings of Israel had a reputation for loyalty and that these advisors at least think that that may be true of Ahab.

Ahab's reply to the message from Ben-hadad has its own subtlety (20:32). The messengers make two points, to which Ahab responds in reverse order. This gives the exchange a carefully balanced, chiastic order:

The messengers say,

(a) *"Your servant,* Ben-hadad, has said,
(b)   'May my spirit *live.'"*[18]

Ahab replies,

(b') "Is-he-still *alive?*
(a') He-is *my-brother."*

(Note that Ahab's reply, like his deft retort in 20:11, is only four words long in Hebrew.)

---

[17] The *NRSV* translates this in the plural: "Their gods are gods of the hills." Either translation is possible. Grammatically the Hebrew word *'ĕlōhîm* is a plural word, "gods," and it is used that way frequently in reference, for instance, to "other gods." However, despite its plural form it is also used regularly as the ordinary way to refer to YHWH as the God (singular) of Israel. The translator must decide whether to reflect in English the presumed point of view of the polytheistic Aramean advisors ("gods") or that of the monotheistic Israelite audience ("God").

[18] Author's translation; *NRSV:* "Your servant Ben-hadad says, 'Please let me live.'"

By countering "your servant" with "my brother," Ahab dismisses Ben-hadad's readiness to accept a subservient position and insists on treating him as an equal. The narrator emphasizes how Ben-hadad's servants seize that nuance and ratify it immediately: "Now the men were watching for an omen; they quickly took it up from him and said, 'Yes, Ben-hadad is your brother'" (20:33). Is there a hint here that Ahab's rhetoric may have outstripped his prudence? The Arameans have certainly gotten better than they bargained for. Has Ahab surrendered something important without realizing it? The narrator plants a small doubt in the reader's mind; it will not long lie dormant.

Ahab reconfirms his intention when Ben-hadad approaches him. Instead of waiting for some gesture of obeisance, Ahab brings Ben-hadad up into his chariot—that is, into his own private royal space, and onto the same level as Ahab. There is, in Hebrew, an ominous echo here. Literally what Ahab does is to make Ben-hadad "go up" into the chariot—the same verb that was used for both of Ben-hadad's attacks on Israel: He "went up against Samaria" (20:1; *NRSV* "marched"), and he "went up to Aphek" (20:26). Neither of those moves succeeded, but now Ahab, who thwarted Ben-hadad's two previous "goings up," freely invites him to "go up" to Ahab himself. Again the narrator seems to be sending subtle signals that something is wrong here. Ahab's lenient treatment of Ben-hadad may prove to be a mistake.

The ambiguity in the narrator's treatment of Ahab continues. The dialogue between Ben-hadad and Ahab is blurred by a vagueness of pronouns that the *NRSV* takes pains to clarify.[19] Literally rendered, 20:34 reads:

> And he said to him, The cities which my father took from your father
> I will return, and you will set up your own markets in Damascus, just
> as my father set up in Samaria. And I, I will send you away with a
> treaty. And he cut with him a treaty and sent him away.

Who said what to whom? We surmise, since the speaker is making concessions, that Ben-hadad, the defeated, is speaking to Ahab, the victor. But that is not confirmed until we reach the word "Damascus." More startling still is the emphatic pronoun "I" toward the end of the verse. Apparently the speaker is now Ahab; Ben-hadad could not reasonably offer to "send

---

[19] Note how the *NRSV* specifies "Ben-hadad" at the beginning of the verse and inserts the words "The king of Israel responded" later in the verse. While these identifications of the speakers are no doubt correct, they are not present in the Hebrew text.

you away" with a treaty. But that is an inference on our part. The Hebrew text gives no overt indication of a change of speaker.[20]

This scene of negotiations sends mixed signals about Ahab. On the surface we see a very positive portrayal of a victor who, unlike his adversary, does not allow power to become tyranny. He treats his enemy graciously, without vindictiveness, and agrees to a treaty aimed at a regional balance of power. At the same time the narrator insinuates some doubts. Is Ahab's restraint politically prudent? Will his generosity toward Ben-hadad end hostilities or not? Is "balance of power" an adequate means to protect the uniqueness of YHWH's covenanted people? When, in the terms of the treaty, Ahab gains reciprocal trading rights in Damascus "as my father did in Samaria," is this an indication that Ahab's Israel is becoming indistinguishable from its Gentile neighbor? Is the fog of pronouns the narrator's way of warning us that, at the end of the day, it's getting hard to tell the two kings apart?

20:35-43

Even these innuendoes cannot prepare us for the unexpected twist the narrative takes in 20:35-43. The treaty of 20:34 brought the Aramean war narrative to apparent closure. What follows seems unrelated at first—and, indeed, there will be no sign of its connection to the Aramean war story for the first third of the episode. The scene starts oddly. With no explanation, one prophet commands another prophet to hit him![21] Even more oddly, this action goes nowhere, narratively speaking: The second prophet refuses, is cursed by the first prophet, departs, and is killed as the curse specified.[22] The action then starts over again, with the first prophet commanding another confrère to hit him. When this one obliges, the first prophet masks himself with a bandage and sets out to wait for the king. We surmise from the context, though it is not stated, that the king is returning home after the battle of Aphek and the conclusion of his treaty with Ben-hadad.

[20] Perhaps the unnecessary and therefore emphatic pronoun is a clue. If so, a reasonable paraphrase might be "and I, for my part, will . . . ."

[21] The verb is a very common word for hitting or striking, and so does not carry any particular nuance of extreme violence or wounding. In the immediate context, however, the verb has appeared frequently in the Aramean war story, always with very strong meaning (*NRSV:* 20:20, "killed"; 20:21: "attacked," "defeated," "great defeat"; 20:29, "killed"). And the second person the prophet asks to hit him will do so strongly enough to wound (20:37). The prophet's undertaking is no symbolic formality, but a matter of utmost seriousness.

[22] Our particular interest in this story lies in what it tells us about Ahab. On a broader contextual level, however, the many resonances between this story and that in 1 Kings 13:10-32 are worth exploring.

The prophet, posing as a soldier wounded in Ahab's service, calls upon the king—as any citizen had a right to do—for judgment on a legal matter. He alleges a case in which he has been accused of neglect, and presents a defense that is, to say the least, flimsy. With the rhetorical flair we've seen him exhibit before, Ahab renders his verdict succinctly (four words in Hebrew, one of them unnecessary and emphatic): "Thus your-judgment: You-decided-it yourself." The prophet then springs his trap. He tears off his bandage, revealing himself (presumably by some sign we no longer know about—a professional tattoo? a tonsure?) as a prophet, his subterfuge as an allegory, and Ahab's verdict as unwittingly self-directed.[23] In YHWH's name he accuses Ahab of violating God's ban on Ben-hadad by freeing him, and he condemns Ahab and his people to the fate Ben-hadad should have suffered.

There are a few clues in the presentation of the case that might have tipped Ahab off to what was going on. First, where was the plaintiff? Under normal circumstances a plaintiff, not a defendant, would bring a case for judgment. The plaintiff's absence might have led Ahab to suspect that the man before him was not, in fact, a defendant but a disguised representative of the true plaintiff, YHWH. Second, the obvious thinness of the alleged defendant's excuses could have suggested that he has a hidden agenda. Finally, the prophet affords Ahab a single positive clue to the subterfuge. He claims that the penalty his comrade attached to the prisoner's escape is "a talent of silver." That is roughly equivalent to the price of a hundred slaves, not just one (see Exod 21:32) and indicates that the "prisoner" (allegorically, Ben-hadad) was no ordinary captive. Ahab, however, misses all the signs. Again we can wonder whether he has substituted clever rhetoric for cautious reflection.

Ahab, surprisingly, is silent in the face of the prophet's condemnation; he says nothing either in his own defense or in retaliation. He simply continues home, "resentful and sullen," as the *NRSV* puts it, or, more accurately, "fuming and furious" (the Hebrew words connote both stubborn resistance and hot anger).

How are we to take this sudden and unprepared divine condemnation? How can we make unified sense of a story that presents Ahab as favored by YHWH, obedient to God's commands, blessed with victory against overwhelming odds, and then, without warning, condemns him for disobedience? The first step is to recognize two different narrative voices, one

---

[23] For the attentive reader there is an inescapable echo of the scene where Nathan tricks David into self-condemnation (2 Sam 12:1-12). The echo points up the stark difference between David's reply, which is a humble confession of sin (2 Sam 12:13), and Ahab's "resentful and sullen" silence (1 Kgs 20:43).

strongly favorable to Ahab, the other strongly critical. For one narrator the relationship between Ahab and YHWH is unproblematically positive; for the other, Ahab's mercy toward Ben-hadad makes a lie of his loyalty to YHWH. Recognizing conflicting narrative voices, however, only partially resolves the problem: It can explain the dissonance in the text, but it cannot explain the text as a *coherent* whole. To do so, we must attend to the unity (the "author") behind the dissonance (the narrators), and ask how the author has positioned those narrative voices with respect to one another and how the author's single message emerges from the tension between the narrators' views.

The first, positively inclined narrator tells us a coherent, unified story in 20:1-34. It is symmetrically constructed and reaches satisfying closure with the treaty of 20:34. There is nothing in the story that clearly foreshadows the surprising developments in 20:35-43. By contrast, the second, negatively inclined narrator does not tell a self-contained story. To condemn Ahab for allowing Ben-hadad to go free presumes the first narrator's tale of the treaty in 20:34. The second narrator, then, is aware of the first story and tells the episode of prophetic condemnation in order to counteract the positive impression the first story can give. The *author,* therefore, does not present these two voices as alternatives on an equal footing. The first narrator's positive view is subordinated to the corrections of the second's negative evaluation. The relative brevity of the negative passage is counterbalanced by its position *after* the positive story, where it casts its condemnatory shadow back on everything that has preceded.[24]

But the author's view cannot simply be equated with the negative narrator's: otherwise there would be no point to creating a positive narrative voice in tension with it. The unifying view of the text is complex and nuanced, and emerges from within that tension. If the final evaluation of Ahab in this chapter is negative—and it is—it is reached only after a lengthy appreciation of the king's military and political accomplishments on the international stage. That those accomplishments are attributed to

---

[24] If the negative narrative voice knows of, and corrects, the story of the positive narrative voice, it may also be that some of its corrections are *inserted* into the positive story and not only appended to it. In 20:1-34 there are no overt interruptions by the negative narrator, but there may be concealed ones. Consider, for instance, the mention of the falling wall that kills twenty-seven thousand Arameans (20:30a). This plays no part in the plot development of 20:1-34; the first narrator's story would not be noticeably different without it. It does, however, allude to the conquest of Jericho (Josh 6:20) and to the ḥerem, or holy war ban, that was imposed on Jericho (Josh 6:17-21; the *NRSV* translates ḥerem as "devoted to destruction"). This lays the groundwork for the prophet's condemnation of Ahab in the second narrator's story, since the condemnation is based on his alleged violation of such a ban (20:42: ". . . you have let the man go whom I had devoted to destruction" [literally, "the man of my ḥerem"]).

divine favor in no way lessens the admiration for a king whose obedience merits such favor. The author does not hide his respect for Ahab or allow it to disappear in the face of his ultimately negative judgment; rather, he keeps approval and disapproval in tension, each moderating the other. The prophetic condemnation reminds the reader that the first narrator's positive picture is not all there is to be said about Ahab. At the same time, the absence of any explicit command to Ahab putting Ben-hadad under the ban subtly weakens its persuasive force by allowing us to wonder whether the condemnation is entirely justified.[25]

The recognition of two conflicting narrative voices in 1 Kings 20 alerts us to attend to the same possibility in the following chapters. It also raises the question whether the author may have used the same narrative device also in the preceding chapters. We shall suggest later that this may indeed be the case.

Chapter 21: The Judicial Murder of an Israelite Landowner

First Kings 22 will begin with a chronological note that, after three years of peace, hostilities broke out again between Aram and Israel. It is during the peaceful interim that we are to situate chapter 21, which describes a series of internal events in Ahab's kingdom. Like chapter 20, chapter 21 comprises a self-contained story about Ahab (21:1-16) and a story of prophetic condemnation (21:17-29) that presumes the preceding story and gives its meaning a new twist. Unlike chapter 20, chapter 21 does not contain pro-Ahab and anti-Ahab narrative voices in tension with each other; both parts of chapter 21 depict Ahab negatively. This, as we shall see, does not preclude the possibility of multiple narrative voices that are each anti-Ahab, but for different reasons. We will examine the self-contained story first, then expand our view to include the story of prophetic condemnation.

---

[25] This is not to deny that the prophet's oracle of condemnation comes from YHWH. The whole point of the abortive episode in 20:35-36 is to demonstrate that the prophet truly speaks God's word and wields God's power. But the author's view is no more to be identified with that of the character called "God" than it is with that of any other character in the narrative. The author here hints very quietly that, while his own overall evaluation of Ahab is negative, he has some reservations about the judgment that Ahab violated the ban by freeing Ben-hadad. Note that, although the narrator's voice confirms the prophet's credentials in general, it nowhere confirms that *this* word accurately conveys a divine message. Later we will see other examples of words and deeds on the part of the character "God" whose ethical quality can give us pause.

21:1-16

In 21:1-16 the narrator uses a powerful literary device to draw the reader into the process of constructing the character of Ahab: ambiguity. The narrator does not usually inform us of Ahab's inner life—his thoughts, feelings, and motivations. Yet much of the action of the story occurs as a result of what Ahab says and does. To what extent is Ahab aware of how his words and deeds will affect events? How one answers that question will greatly shape the character one attributes to Ahab. We will point up the ambiguities as we examine the story; once we have worked our way through 21:1-16 we will see what possibilities those ambiguities open up for understanding the character of Ahab.

The first characterization of Ahab is easily overlooked. The narrator tells us that he is "King of Samaria" (21:1), and that he has a palace in Jezreel.[26] The title "King of Samaria" is very rare in the Hebrew Bible, occurring only here and in 2 Kings 1:3, where it describes Ahab's son Ahaziah. The Hebrew Bible usually refers to the northern kingdom as "Israel," not "Samaria,"[27] and to its king as "King of Israel" (as, for instance, in 21:18: "Ahab, king of Israel, who [is] in Samaria"). The use of the unusual title here awakens several connotations. It emphasizes Ahab's connection with the capital city rather than with the nation as a whole. Since Samaria had no roots in Israelite tradition (it was founded fresh by Ahab's father, Omri, as a new capital for the country; see 16:24), and, more importantly, since this was where Ahab himself built a temple and an altar for Baal (16:32), styling Ahab "King of Samaria" evokes thoughts of his distance from Israelite and Yahwistic ways, and specifically of his attachment to the worship of Baal that was the constant issue in chapters 17–19. It also reminds the reader that Ahab's primary residence was in his capital, and that the plot of land at issue—the vineyard of Naboth the Jezreelite—was adjacent not to Ahab's main royal palace but to a secondary residence in Jezreel.[28]

[26] Samaria, the capital city of Israel, was located in the hill country of central Palestine, in the tribal territory of Manasseh, at the site known today as Sebastiya. It was founded by Ahab's father, Omri (1 Kgs 16:24). Extensive archaeological investigations have unearthed impressive remains from the time of Omri and Ahab, but very little evidence of earlier occupation. The city of Jezreel was located farther north, in the eastern portion of the fertile Valley of Jezreel (also called the Plain of Esdraelon), in the tribal territory of Issachar; this site, known today as Zerin, has been archaeologically surveyed, but not excavated.

[27] During the Assyrian period (after 722 B.C.E.) the term "Samaria" was extended to refer to the whole Assyrian province of which the city of Samaria was the capital. This was roughly equivalent to the old Israelite tribal territories of Ephraim and Manasseh.

[28] Scholars are unsure of the significance of this secondary residence. Some think it was a seasonal palace for use during the winter months, since the valley location would have been warmer than the hill of Samaria.

The action begins with a dialogue between Ahab and Naboth. The details of this conversation are important because echoes of it will recur several times in the course of the chapter, and variations in those echoes will tell us much about the character of Ahab. Ahab wishes to purchase Naboth's vineyard and turn it into a kitchen garden for the royal residence. On the surface of it this is reasonable; its proximity to the palace would make it convenient for the king's household. On the other hand, to uproot an established vineyard in order to plant a vegetable garden tacitly trivializes the years of effort that must be invested to bring a vineyard to productivity. The king makes what seems to be a fair proposal: His first offer is land for land, since this is most likely to appeal to a landowner who makes his livelihood from his property. Indeed, Ahab even offers a "better vineyard" in exchange. In case Naboth finds that proposal unacceptable, Ahab offers as an alternative the vineyard's value in silver.[29] Naboth's reply is abrupt and definitive. He uses two telling phrases that make it clear that he is not simply bargaining for a better price; his decision is not negotiable. First, he uses a religious phrase indicating that it would be sacrilegious for him to sell his vineyard: *ḥālîlâ lî mêyhwh* (literally "profanation to me from YHWH"; *NRSV:* "The LORD forbid"). Second, he explains why selling it would be sacrilegious: The vineyard is his "ancestral inheritance"—that is, the landholding granted specifically to his family by God. That land, unlike other property, could not be bought and sold except in dire emergency.[30] In short, Naboth does not *refuse* Ahab's proposal so much as plead that, on religious and legal grounds, he *cannot* sell Ahab the vineyard. The fact that Ahab does not pursue the matter further argues that he understands these implications.

It does not, however, mean that Ahab *accepts* the implications! He returns home "resentful and sullen"—exactly the same phrase that described his reaction to the prophetic condemnation four verses previously (20:43). As was mentioned above, the connotations of those two terms in Hebrew bespeak stubborn resistance and hot anger; "fuming and furious" captures

[29] Technically the *NRSV*'s "money" can be misleading here. Coinage, as a standardized medium of exchange, only begins to appear in the Israelite environment during the Persian period (late sixth to fourth centuries B.C.E.). In Ahab's day (ninth century B.C.E.) silver would have been weighed out in payment.

[30] The "ancestral inheritance" was the land that belonged to each family as its patrimony. It was understood theologically as God's gift to the family (just as the Promised Land was understood as God's gift to the whole people). The ancestral inheritance could be sold only if the family was so destitute that it could not survive otherwise. Even then it could only be sold temporarily, until the next jubilee year, when all such property reverted to its original owners. These practices are codified in the laws of Leviticus 25:23-28. Although these laws are probably later than the text of 1 Kings 21, they enshrine earlier traditions that would have been familiar to the author and original audience of our passage.

the nuances better than "resentful and sullen." The terms intimate, first, that Ahab is not ready to consider the case closed and, second, that his anger is not cold and contained ("sullen") but boiling and raging.

As Ahab makes his way home, he repeats Naboth's words to himself: "I will not give you my ancestral inheritance."[31] Interior monologue—that is, a person deliberating internally—is generally a very reliable index of character, since when we talk to ourselves we most often say what we truly think and feel. It is revealing to consider how closely Ahab recalls what Naboth said. He quotes the technical phrase "ancestral inheritance" accurately, but leaves out (forgets? ignores?) Naboth's religious protest, *ḥālîlâ lî mêyhwh*. Instead he substitutes a simple refusal: "I will not give." Where it touches on matters of Israelite legal tradition, Ahab acknowledges the grounds for Naboth's decision; but when it comes to YHWH's approval or disapproval all that matters to Ahab is that he is not getting his own way.

Arriving home, Ahab behaves like a petulant child: He retires to his rooms and refuses to eat. His wife, Jezebel, reads his mood accurately[32] and questions its source. Ahab recounts his interview with Naboth, but modifies both his own original proposal and Naboth's response. Where to Naboth he had first offered land ("a *better* vineyard") and silver as an alternative, he now tells Jezebel that he first offered silver, with land ("*another* vineyard") as an alternative. In repeating Naboth's answer he leaves out (as he did already in 21:4) the religious exclamation *ḥālîlâ lî mêyhwh;* but now he also replaces "ancestral inheritance" with "my vineyard," an ordinary reference that carries none of the legal weight of the technical term. Here we encounter narrative gaps that produce a first set of ambiguities in the chapter. Why does Ahab revise the wording of his discussion with Naboth? Are his changes innocent and his sulking mere pique, or is there a deeper agenda behind them? The narrator gives us no insight into Ahab's motives. We will explore the possibilities in a moment.

Jezebel's attendance on Ahab shows one side of her character: that she is truly concerned about her spouse and his happiness. Her comment on what he tells her, however, shows another side as well. Her remark: "Do

---

[31] There is a peculiarity in the Hebrew here that most English translations ignore. The last words of 21:5 read, literally, "and he said," not "for he had said," as the *NRSV* has it. According to the normal rules of Hebrew prose syntax the subject "he" refers to Ahab, not to Naboth, yet the words that follow reprise Naboth's words. One can make sense of the text as it stands only by understanding that Ahab is speaking, but that he is muttering Naboth's words to himself as he replays their conversation in his mind.

[32] She uses *sar*, one of the adjectives the narrator used in 21:4, although the *NRSV* chooses to translate it differently in the two places ("resentful" in 21:4 and "depressed" in 21:5).

you now govern [literally, "exercise kingship over"] Israel?" drips with sarcasm: "What kind of king are you anyway?" In the larger context of the concern she has just expressed, the sarcasm does not seem to reflect scorn and contempt for Ahab so much as frustration with his failure to be the sort of king she thinks he ought to be. Her remark is also unconsciously ironic, since in order to console her husband, *she* will wield the king's name and seal, demonstrating that she can "exercise kingship" more effectively than he does.

Ahab is absent from 21:8-14 except in the narrator's remark that Jezebel's conspiratorial letter was written "in Ahab's name and sealed . . . with his seal." Again we have a gap and an ambiguity: Is Ahab aware that Jezebel has appropriated his royal authority? If he is not, then we have a weak king behind whose back the real power of the kingdom is wielded. On the other hand, if he *is* aware, then we have a king who lets others carry out his dirty work for him and tacitly approves whatever they do in the process. However one reads it, the king is undeserving of admiration, but the two different readings produce substantially different understandings of the king's character.

After Naboth has been killed, Jezebel tells Ahab that Naboth is dead (though she neglects to mention that he was executed for "cursing God and the king"!), and tells him to take possession of the vineyard. Ahab says nothing; he simply does what he is told to do. Is he puzzled at this convenient death? Is he interested in how it happened? Does he wonder how Jezebel learned of it? Does he question why the "ancestral inheritance" need no longer remain in Naboth's family?[33] Again the narrator shows us nothing of his interior thoughts and thereby leaves us free to fill the gaps in the tale by our own speculation.

There are at least two ways to discern a coherent character sketch of Ahab in this story; each of them fills the narrative gaps and resolves the ambiguities differently, and thereby produces a quite different reading of the king. Both are plausible. The effect of the text, then, is to offer us alternative negative portrayals of Ahab[34] but not to impose either of them.

---

[33] This may be a puzzle for modern scholars more than for Ahab, by virtue of our ignorance of the details of Israelite property law. There is nothing in the laws of the Hebrew Bible that would justify royal seizure of the "ancestral inheritance." Some scholars conjecture that Naboth died without heirs, and that in such cases the state inherited the property; this opinion grows out of the desire to harmonize 1 Kings 21 with 2 Kings 9:26, which claims that Naboth's sons were killed along with him. Others speculate that in cases where someone was executed for *lèse majesté* ("Naboth cursed God and the king") the criminal's property was confiscate to the offended crown.

[34] And of Jezebel! For a further exploration of Jezebel see Patricia Dutcher-Walls, *Jezebel: Portraits of a Queen,* Interfaces (Collegeville: Liturgical Press, 2004).

First, and most simply, Ahab's petulance may be exactly that: the childish pouting of someone balked of what he wants. His adaptations of the conversation with Naboth reflect what he thinks will interest his wife and win her sympathy. As he recounts to Jezebel his offer to Naboth he says that first he offered silver, then, as an alternative, another (not a "better") vineyard. Jezebel is a queen, and was raised as a princess;[35] she is not a commoner and has never been dependent on crops for her livelihood. Ahab believes that silver will be more meaningful to her than land. His insight into Jezebel's character is accurate: Later, when Jezebel recalls Ahab's account in 21:15, she remembers the offer of silver, but not that of land for land. Moreover, it seems likely that in other countries royal will was law; if the king wanted a particular piece of land, he simply took it in return for whatever compensation he deemed sufficient.[36] For Ahab to tell his foreign-born spouse that he *negotiated* with Naboth is already to invite her scorn; to admit that he offered Naboth a *better* vineyard in return would be, Ahab fears, to demean himself in her eyes. In this too he is quite justified, as her sarcastic retort makes clear.

When Ahab repeats Naboth's answer, he continues to leave out Naboth's religious argument, as he did when speaking to himself in 21:4. Even if Ahab remembers Naboth's words correctly, his Baalist queen would not be concerned with what a Yahwist would consider profanation. However, Ahab now also leaves out the term that invokes Israelite legal traditions, "ancestral inheritance," thinking perhaps that such technical arguments will make no sense to his Sidonian spouse. If this is his reasoning, he is quite wrong. The plot Jezebel hatches in 21:9-10 is meticulous in its conformity to both cultic and legal requirements and demonstrates that Jezebel had a familiarity with Israelite law much greater than one would expect.

Jezebel then, on her own initiative and probably unknown to Ahab, develops the conspiracy that will eventuate in Naboth's death. While Ahab sulks, feeling sorry for himself, Jezebel forges letters, corrupts officials, suborns witnesses, and compasses Naboth's execution. When her plans bear fruit, Jezebel presents Ahab with the vineyard. He, in turn, like a child with a new toy, doesn't question where it came from—all he cares about is that he now owns it.

In this reading of the story Jezebel is the true villain. Ahab is weak and spoiled, especially by comparison with his decisive, devious, and un-

---

[35] Jezebel's father was Ethbaal (or Ittobaal), king of Sidon; see 16:31.

[36] It must be admitted, however, that our knowledge of surrounding cultures, such as Jezebel's Sidon, is very limited. It is quite conceivable that other cultures besides Israel set limits to royal power that are not reflected in the sparse evidence that has come down to us.

scrupulous queen. Her evil is abuse of power, corruption of law, and judicial murder; his evil is culpable ignorance.

The alternative reading, however, sees a quite different Ahab. Let us begin from the observation that, when all is said and done, *Ahab gets what he wants.* Jezebel's concern for Ahab's mood suggests that she reads him well and is responsive to his needs. Conversely, the way Ahab rewords the offer he made to Naboth suggests that Ahab also reads Jezebel well, and knows what will and what will not move her. It may well be that Ahab's behavior is not simply a play for sympathy, but rather a contrived campaign to manipulate Jezebel to action: His fuming elicits her concern, his refusal to eat evokes her question about what has happened, his revision of the offer to Naboth plays to her prejudices, and his account of Naboth's refusal gains her promise to "make everything better." In recounting his own words to Naboth, Ahab presents things in the way that will make most sense to her. In recounting Naboth's words to him, Ahab leaves out the fact that the land is Naboth's ancestral inheritance not because he thinks Jezebel will be uninterested in that detail but because he is aware that she is familiar with Israelite law (as the details of her conspiracy subsequently show). He does not want her to realize that, as ancestral inheritance, the vineyard was ultimately not alienable, even for the crown.

Jezebel has ready access to the king's seal. Ahab would be fully aware of that, although it seems less likely that he would be aware of the details of Jezebel's plot. Having incited her to act, Ahab simply sits back and lets her do the dirty work. When she brings him the word, he learns all he needs to know: "Naboth is not alive, but dead." He does not ask how it happened; if he is ignorant, he can feign innocence as well. "Deniability" is not a modern invention!

In this reading the true villain is Ahab, who maneuvers Jezebel into a sacrilegious violation of Israelite law and thereby keeps his own hands clean of direct involvement in the crime of judicial murder. He is strong, determined, cunning, and a clever manipulator. Jezebel is not innocent, of course, but primary culpability lies with the king, who uses her as a tool to get what he wants.

The self-contained story of Ahab and Naboth, then, presents us with an unambiguously negative picture of the royal couple. It lays at their feet a crime of judicial murder involving abusive exercise of royal power and callous corruption of Israelite civil, legal, and cultic institutions. However, it does not clearly apportion guilt between the king and queen. Rather, it leaves the reader to decide whether Ahab is a weakling, no match for his powerful and unscrupulous queen, or on the contrary a devious and manipulative man ready to exploit even his own wife's concern for the sake of his own gratification.

21:17-29

In the second half of the chapter the prophet Elijah features more prominently than Ahab. YHWH commissions Elijah to deliver an oracle of condemnation to the king for the crime against Naboth (21:17-19). Besides YHWH's clear disapproval of Ahab, at which we will look more closely in a moment, other, subtler elements in YHWH's speech contribute to the characterization of Ahab. YHWH's first words to Elijah are *qûm rēd* (21:18; literally "Arise! Go down . . .").[37] The words recall Jezebel's very similar imperatives to Ahab three verses earlier: *qûm rēš* (21:15; literally "Arise! Take possession . . ."; *NRSV* "Go, take possession . . ."). The echo establishes an antithetic correlation between Ahab and Elijah: The prophet is not only YHWH's messenger to Ahab; he is also Ahab's narrative counterpoint, antagonist to Ahab's protagonist. YHWH goes on to call Ahab "the king of Israel." Under ordinary circumstances this common title would have no special significance; in the present context, however, Ahab has already been introduced with the unusual phrase "the king *of Samaria*" (21:1; see above, p. 48), and YHWH's next words allude to this earlier title with the unnecessary elaboration "who [is][38] in Samaria." Why this elaboration, especially since Ahab is *not* in Samaria but in Jezreel, as YHWH's next words make plain? Together the title and the elaboration revive the contrast between "Israel" (the country, YHWH's people) and "Samaria" (the capital city, with its Baalist leanings) mentioned earlier, and point to the fact that the one who is (or at least should be) the "king of Israel" in fact inhabits Baalist Samaria. The significance of reminding the reader about Ahab's Baalism will emerge only when we consider the chapter as a whole below (see p. 64).

YHWH's speech to Elijah continues with two very formal oracular pronouncements, both of which Elijah is commissioned to deliver with a messenger formula: "You shall say to him, 'Thus says the LORD . . . .'" The first pronouncement specifies the crime with a rhetorical question: "Have you killed and also taken possession?"[39] The second imposes sentence for the crime, using a formulation that recalls talionic law (that is, the punish-

---

[37] The *NRSV* correctly translates simply "Go down . . . ." In Hebrew the *qûm* is idiomatic and does not have literal force here; it is rather like the verb "come" in the American colloquialism, "Come on, let's go . . . ." Nevertheless, the word is there, and its presence helps establish the echo spoken of above.

[38] YHWH's elaboration is both unnecessary and somewhat awkward. When, as here, there is no verb expressed in a Hebrew sentence like this, the copulative "is" must be supplied. But in fact Ahab is not at the moment in Samaria but in Jezreel, where he has gone to take possession of Naboth's vineyard. This is why the *NRSV* inserts "rules" here instead of "is": It smooths out the awkwardness without seriously distorting the meaning.

[39] In Hebrew the question benefits from extremely terse wording and dense sound-play: *hărāṣaḥtā wĕgam-yārāštā*. The assonance of the two verbs links them extremely closely, so

ment fits the crime).[40] The talionic character is twofold: Ahab's punishment will occur in the same place and in the same manner (dogs licking up the blood) as Naboth's death. Both oracles identify the crime as the judicial murder of Naboth and the seizure of his property, and both focus on Ahab's culpability, with no mention of Jezebel.

When Elijah encounters Ahab, the king greets him oddly: "Have you found me, O my enemy?" In these few words (only two words in Hebrew; Ahab still has his flair for powerful, concise rhetoric), multiple levels of meaning resound. Ahab knows that Elijah seeks him and, apparently, Ahab is not happy to be found. He knows that their relationship in general is a hostile one ("O my enemy"), but in the immediate context Ahab's defensiveness betrays his guilty conscience.[41] He knows that Elijah comes with condemnation and that he, Ahab, deserves it. In this way Ahab's own voice joins forces with YHWH's to lay primary guilt on the king rather than on the queen.

Behind the voice of Ahab we can also discern the voice of the narrator, reminding us of earlier scenes. In chapter 18 Obadiah revealed how *Ahab* had been seeking *Elijah,* and with no friendly intent (18:10). In Ahab's opinion Elijah was the "troubler of Israel" (18:17), responsible for the drought that was devastating the people. Now that the tables are turned and Elijah is seeking him, Ahab can no longer hide the guilt of his

---

that the killing and the taking possession are almost two sides of the same coin; perhaps a comparable effect in English might be felt in "Have you murdered then plundered?" Further, the Hebrew verb *yāraš* has a range of meaning that stretches from "take possession [by inheritance]" to "take possession [by seizure]," and thus can accommodate both the violent usurpation of Naboth's vineyard and whatever legal loophole enabled the crown to lay claim to what had once been Naboth's "ancestral inheritance."

[40] The term comes from the so-called "law of talion": "an eye for an eye, a tooth for a tooth." This was one of the fundamental principles of Israelite law; see, for example, Exodus 21:22-25; Leviticus 24:19-20; Deuteronomy 19:21. This principle is often misunderstood today. It does not exalt vengeance, but restricts it: It limits how much punishment can be imposed on the guilty. One cannot exact a penalty more serious than the offense. Furthermore, there are numerous indications within the Hebrew Bible that the law of talion was not intended as a literal prescription, so that the guilty party would suffer the same physical damage as the offended party, but as a guideline for the level of compensation, monetary or otherwise, that the guilty party was liable for. The principle is often alluded to in prophetic passages where crime and punishment are expressed in identical vocabulary. In the nearby context, for instance, although the *NRSV* obscures the echo, Ahab is condemned for "doing evil" [*NRSV:* "do what is evil," 21:20]; his punishment is that YHWH will "bring evil" [*NRSV:* "bring disaster," 21:21] upon him.

[41] For a powerful meditation on the whole story of Naboth and, in particular, on the culpability of Ahab, see Davie Napier, "The Inheritance and the Problem of Adjacency: An Essay on I Kings 21," *Interpretation* 30 (1976) 3–11, published also in his *Word of God, Word of Earth* (Philadelphia: United Church Press, 1976) 76–87.

wrongdoing behind a façade of concern for others; he knows that any coming condemnation is his own responsibility. Another allusion hides in the words as well. In 17:18, after the death of her son, the widow of Zarephath upbraided Elijah, "What have you against me, O man of God? You have come to me to bring my sin to remembrance, and to cause the death of my son." Like the widow, Ahab sees Elijah as the bearer of disaster; unlike the widow, however, Ahab deserves the disaster, and knows it. The very way they address Elijah reflects their different characters: The widow identifies Elijah in terms of his divine calling ("man of God"); Ahab describes him only in terms of how he relates to Ahab ("my enemy"). Ultimately the widow's son was returned to life; Ahab's son will be condemned to death.

Elijah's response begins by repeating the first significant word of Ahab's question: "I have found you." This is the standard Hebrew fashion for saying "yes"; it not only answers Ahab's question but also implies that Ahab's description of Elijah as his "enemy" is accurate. Elijah's speech continues with a double oracle in ABB'A' pattern: crime, punishment, punishment, crime. The first pair uses very general terms, the second is more specific; we are no doubt to understand the second pair as spelling out the particulars of the first rather than referring to a second and separate crime-and-punishment. The first crime Elijah cites is that Ahab has "sold himself to do evil";[42] his punishment, according to Elijah, is that YHWH will "bring evil [*NRSV:* disaster]" upon him. The formulation is talionic (see n. 40 above), but entirely vague. The "evil" that will come upon Ahab is spelled out next (21:21aβ-22a), in detailed terms that will be familiar to the experienced reader of 1 Kings from the earlier stories of Jeroboam and Baasha.[43] YHWH will "consume" Ahab (compare 1 Kings 14:10b and 16:3a),[44] he will "cut off every male" of Ahab's family (compare 14:10a), and he will "make his

---

[42] The idiom "to sell oneself" can be misleading in English. Although drawn from the realm of commerce, the metaphor is not one of cost-benefit ratio, as in "Ahab gave up his integrity and got Naboth's vineyard in exchange." Rather, it is simply one of delivering goods, as in "Ahab gave himself over to doing evil"; it does not imply that there was a concrete return (such as the vineyard) for the goods delivered.

[43] Jeroboam and Baasha were the founders of the first two dynasties to rule the northern kingdom. In their cases YHWH's sentence decreed the end of their dynasties; both kings were succeeded by a son, but the son's reign in each case was cut short by assassination and coup d'état after two years. In Ahab's case he is not the founder of the dynasty; that was his father, Omri. YHWH's sentence therefore decrees the destruction of *Ahab's* line (this will occur in 2 Kings 9–11), but not necessarily of the entire Omrid dynasty.

[44] The intent of the Hebrew metaphor is clear—it means that Ahab (and his lineage) will be wiped out—though the precise literal meaning of the terms is disputed. What is important for our analysis is that all three passages use exactly the same terminology. This clear echo justifies using the three passages to illuminate each other.

house like the house of Jeroboam son of Nebat and like the house of Baasha son of Ahijah" (compare 16:3b). And the crime is similarly described in familiar terms from the same contexts: "You have provoked me [i.e., YHWH] to anger and caused Israel to sin" (compare 14:9, 15b-16 and 15:34; 16:2b).

It is noteworthy that nothing in Elijah's double oracle corresponds in any evident way to the double oracle YHWH commissioned him to deliver in 21:19. YHWH and his prophet speak with very different voices. On the one hand, in Elijah's words to Ahab there is no reference to the crime against Naboth on which YHWH's condemnation focused. It would certainly be possible to understand that crime as the deed that "provoked [YHWH] to anger," especially in view of YHWH's condemnation in 21:19, and the suborning of Jezreel's elders as what "caused Israel to sin" (though, according to 21:1-16, this was Jezebel's deed, not Ahab's), but the verbal allusions to the parallel condemnations of Jeroboam and Baasha point in a very different direction. Jeroboam's crime that "provoked YHWH to anger" and "led Israel into sin" was the establishment of sanctuaries at Dan and Bethel in which a golden calf was the central cult object.[45] In fact, that became paradigmatic for the sinfulness of the northern kingdom; in 1–2 Kings virtually every king of the northern kingdom is condemned for continuing "the sin of Jeroboam" (see 16:31 for Ahab's condemnation on this basis). Baasha's "evil" is the same: he "walked in the way of Jeroboam" (15:34 and 16:2).

On the other hand, Elijah's condemnation of Ahab goes far beyond what we see YHWH authorizing in 21:17-19. YHWH's words contain no mention of punishment of Ahab's descendants or obliteration of his lineage. There is certainly precedent in Israelite prophetic tradition for the prophet's right to rephrase, adapt, or even expand the divine word he is commissioned to speak. Here, however, the differences between what YHWH tells Elijah to say and what Elijah actually says are so dramatic that we are entitled to wonder whether the prophet may not be exceeding his mandate.[46] One telling detail is that, even though Elijah speaks in YHWH's name (i.e., he uses "I" to mean YHWH in 21:21-22), he does *not* introduce

---

[45] As it is presented in 1 Kings the cult at these sanctuaries was idolatrous, and the golden calf was an idol that people worshiped (see 12:28-30). Historically, this is probably not accurate. It is more likely that the golden calf was understood by its devotees as a seat or footstool for YHWH, invisibly enthroned above it. (Compare the cherubim—most likely winged lions with human faces—on top of the Ark of the Covenant, which were understood as supporting YHWH's invisible divine throne in the Temple at Jerusalem.) The misrepresentation is likely due to the Judean author's contempt for (or at least ignorance of) the religious practices of the northern kingdom.

[46] See Jesse C. Long, Jr., *1 & 2 Kings*, The College Press NIV Commentary (Joplin, MO: College Press, 2002) 255–56.

what he says with the messenger formula ("Thus says YHWH") as prophets regularly do, and as YHWH explicitly instructed him to.

In short, YHWH and his prophet not only speak with very different voices; they also seem to see Ahab with rather different eyes. YHWH's concern is with judicial murder, unjust seizure of property, and punishment appropriate to the crime. The issues in Elijah's pronouncement are a demand for exclusive worship of YHWH and the dynastic doom that violation of that demand entails.

At first glance Elijah's concern for exclusive Yahwism might seem to converge with his attitudes in 1 Kings 17–19, where he campaigned so mightily against the worship of Baal. There is, however, a fundamental difference. In 1 Kings 17–19 Elijah's consistent target was Baalism. The proclamation of a drought (challenging Baal's claim to be the god of storms and vegetation), the enmity of Jezebel (proponent of Baalism and persecutor of YHWH prophets), the contest with Baal's prophets on Mount Carmel—all point to the unbridgeable chasm between Elijah's exclusivist Yahwism and the cult of Baal, which was tolerant of the worship of other gods (see, for example, 18:21). In 21:21-22, however, the citations of the condemnation of Jeroboam (14:9-11) and Baasha (15:34–16:4) have the calf sanctuaries of Dan and Bethel in view, not the worship of Baal.

It is precisely those citations that point to a still deeper difference. Where in 1 Kings 17–19 we had no reason to doubt the authenticity of Elijah's behavior, here citations of earlier passages from 1 Kings betray the presence of a narratorial voice speaking through the character's words. Compare, for example, the way in which the narrator's voice sounds behind Ahab's in 21:20a (see above, p. 55). In fact, since almost every significant word in Elijah's double oracle appears already in the condemnations of Jeroboam and Baasha, Elijah himself is left with nothing much more than his first word, "I have found you." The narrator actually *co-opts* the rest of Elijah's speech.[47] The depiction of Ahab in 21:21-22, then, represents that of a narrator rather than Elijah, and it should come as no surprise that it differs from the one Elijah projects in chapters 17–19.

---

[47] This is not implausible. Even in the immediate context we can see an example of the narrator "invading," so to speak, a character's utterance. In 21:10 Jezebel writes a letter instructing the elders of Jezreel how to carry out the plot she has devised to accomplish Naboth's death. In that letter she calls the perjurious witnesses "scoundrels"—yet it is hardly likely that she would put such an insulting description of her own lackeys in a letter to her accomplices! A few verses later (21:13) we learn that "scoundrels" is in fact the *narrator's* term for the false witnesses. The narrator's infiltration of Jezebel's words injects both irony (Jezebel knows that her own hirelings are scoundrels) and satire (if Jezebel knowingly enlists scoundrels, what does that say about Jezebel herself?!).

The question of tangled voices becomes even knottier in 21:23-24. Whose voice(s?) do we hear in these verses? There is nothing in Hebrew corresponding to quotation marks in English, and so there is no indication whether Elijah's speech continues in 21:23-24 or the narrator's voice replaces that of the prophet. Our first inclination is to hear Elijah elaborating on the far-reaching destiny he has just decreed in YHWH's name: Jezebel comes in for particularly gruesome punishment, and the graphic image of dogs eating corpses is applied both to her and to the whole doomed household of Ahab. Yet there are elements in these verses that fit more comfortably if these are not Elijah's words but a narrator's. The shift to speaking of YHWH in the third person is unexpected after the consistent use of the first-person pronoun "I" for YHWH in 21:21-22. Also, neither YHWH's words in 21:17-19 nor Elijah's in 21:20-22 mention Jezebel, but she will clearly be the object of a narrator's condemnation in 21:25. Finally, 21:24 is a further citation of the condemnations of Jeroboam and Baasha (compare14:11 and 16:4), which, as we saw above, betrays the presence of the narrator's voice. As in 21:20-21, then, we have two voices overlaid, Elijah's and a narrator's, with Elijah's voice fronting for the narrator, while the latter is more determinative of the point of view the text projects.

The retrospective tone of 21:25-26 leaves no doubt that these utterances are the narrator's. However, the particular narrative technique involved is worth examining. What the narrator says in these verses is not, in and of itself, part of the story. Rather, it is as if the narrator has stepped out of storytelling mode to comment directly to the reader about the story. This sort of aside to the reader (or, technically, to the "narratee"; see above, p. 13) is an example of what is called "breaking frame." Its effects on a reader are subtle but considerable. For one thing, it reminds the reader that the events being narrated are not *present* but *past*. This creates a certain distance between reader and recital, lessens narrative immediacy, and invites a more reflective reading. Sometimes this distance affords the reader an opportunity to perceive subtle connections and allusions to other texts or ideas; sometimes it urges the reader to reexamine and reconstrue what has gone before; sometimes, as here, it introduces an element of moral judgment and critical evaluation about particular characters or events. A quite different effect of breaking frame, though, is its impact on the credulity of the reader. To hear the narrator turn and address us directly gives us a feeling of being "in the know": The one who *really* knows is sharing inside information with us. It is really a subtle appeal to the reader's vanity, an attempt to circumvent the critical ear with which we might otherwise receive the narrator's opinions. Here, for instance, the critical evaluation of Ahab echoes the narrator's comprehensive condemnation in 16:30-33 and implies that the story of the crime against Naboth somehow justifies a condemnation of Ahab for idolatry. Were that claim more overt we would see it for the *non sequitur* it is; the apparent candor of a narrative aside diverts our attention and camouflages the lapse in logic.

What claims about Ahab do these verses make? The first part of 21:25 echoes two earlier judgments: first, the assertion that Ahab's evil was unparalleled in Israel's history (16:30, 33b); second, that Ahab "sold himself to do evil in the sight of the LORD" (21:20; on the idiom see n. 42 above). As in those earlier passages, Ahab's crime is described only with the generic term "evil." Oddly, this extreme censure is immediately compromised in the last words of the verse, which divert responsibility from Ahab to Jezebel. The next verse specifies Ahab's evil (without mention of Jezebel) as idolatry, but the reference is neither to the calf sanctuaries of Jeroboam nor to Baal worship. The term this verse uses for "idols" *(gillulîm)* is never used in the Hebrew Bible of either of those forms of worship. It is used only for the gods of other nations—Egypt, Assyria, Babylon—and especially of the Canaanite peoples (the "Amorites") "whom the LORD drove out before the Israelites." This is an entirely new charge against Ahab, with no basis anywhere in the narrative to this point. There is, however, one subtle verbal allusion in the verse to the crime against Naboth, though it is lost in the *NRSV* translation. The *gillulîm* are the gods of those whom YHWH *dispossessed* (*NRSV*: "drove out"); the Hebrew word is *yāraš*, the same verb YHWH uses to describe Ahab's crime in 21:19a ("Have you killed and also *taken possession?*"). This allusion raises the question whether the charges against Ahab of idolatry and judicial murder may converge at some deeper level; we will pursue this possibility in a moment.

Ahab's response to "those words" (that is, to the words of Elijah in 21:20b-22, not to the narrator's aside in 21:25-26), is a series of classic acts of mourning: He tears his garments, he puts on sackcloth,[48] and he fasts. The last words of 21:27 are unclear. The *NRSV*'s translation "dejectedly" is conjectural. The Hebrew word usually means something like "gentle, quiet, unobtrusive"; it does not mean "dejected" anywhere else in the Hebrew Bible. The meaning may be that Ahab undertook these penitential practices in private, without making any public spectacle of them. Whatever it means, it certainly describes his outward *manner* and does not give any insight into his inner *mood* (as "dejected" would imply). As usual, the

[48] "Sackcloth" (Hebrew *śaq*) is some sort of coarse cloth made from goat hair, camel hair, or the like. A modern equivalent would be burlap. (The similarity to English "sack" is not coincidental; etymologically, "sack" goes back to the Semitic word.) The discomfort of wearing such coarse fabric next to the skin made it appropriate for mourning or penitence. The text goes on to say that Ahab "lay" in sackcloth, implying that he wore it day and night—a practice that would be extreme, but is attested in one other case of dire need (see Joel 1:13).

Ahab in the Ahab Stories: 1 Kings 20–22 | 61

narrator does not allow us any direct insight into Ahab's interior life. We see only what he does; from that we must infer what he is thinking.

The scene ends with another divine word to Elijah, paralleling that with which this part of the story began (21:28 is absolutely identical to 21:17), although in this case the divine word is simply YHWH's comment to Elijah, not a commission for delivery to the king. YHWH is a bit wordy here, unnecessarily repeating that Ahab "has humbled himself before me" and "I will [not] bring the disaster." YHWH is clearly pleased by Ahab's penitential behavior (the verb "to humble oneself" refers to behavior—"subjecting oneself to another"—and not to inner attitudes like "humility"). In response to the king's subjection, YHWH exempts him from punishment (thus negating YHWH's own oracle in 21:19b) and deflects it to his son (thus conforming to Elijah's pronouncements in 21:21-22). About all we can infer about Ahab from YHWH's remarks is that YHWH deems Ahab's penitence sincere and sufficient. There is no indication that Ahab is ever informed of YHWH's leniency.

The complexity of the weave of voices speaking to us of Ahab in 21:17-29 goes well beyond what we saw in chapter 20. In these verses we have YHWH, Ahab himself, and Elijah all presenting views of Ahab for our consideration, plus several narratorial voices whose only point of agreement seems to be antipathy toward the king. Three sets of questions arise. First, how do these voices, with their respective portrayals of Ahab, relate to one another? Is there a hierarchy, so that one voice is subordinated to another (as, in chapter 20, the positive narrator's voice was subordinate to and corrected by the negative voice)? Second, how do they relate to the alternative portrayals we discerned in 21:1-16? Do the various voices and their interrelationships help us fill the narrative gaps, clarify the ambiguities, and choose between the possible constructions of Ahab's character? Finally, can we, in all this plethora of voices, detect a unified and unifying view of Ahab—one that would correspond to an "author," with all the connotations of "authoritative" that word carries?

YHWH's voice is clear: It condemns Ahab for the crime against Naboth. Yet the phrase "who [is] in Samaria" is awkward in this speech, both grammatically and thematically. It alludes to the narrator's words in 21:1, and seems best understood as a *narrator's* intervention into YHWH's speech. (See n. 47 above for another example of this sort of narrative invasion of a character's words.) This suggests, as we would expect, that a character's speech is subordinate to that of a narrator, who can adapt that speech for purposes other than those of the character.[49] In this case the

---

[49] This is not surprising. After all, even a character's speech is reported to us by the narrator who, therefore, controls not only the description of the scene but also the wording of the speech itself.

evocation of Ahab's Baalist allegiances fits the narrator's agenda, though it does not seem to be part of YHWH's. Ahab's two words ("Have-you-found-me, O-my-enemy?") and Elijah's one-word reply ("I-have-found-you") also show signs of narratorial control in the allusions to earlier passages of 1 Kings 17–19 that we mentioned above, allusions that are meaningful to narrator and reader, but hardly so to Ahab and Elijah in their encounter in the vineyard. By themselves Ahab and Elijah affirm their mutual hostility; in the immediate context that hostility must arise from Ahab's crime against Naboth. The narrator's hidden allusion to 18:10, however, colors that hostility with the hues of the polemic against Baal worship that characterizes 1 Kings 17–19.

The remainder of Elijah's speech (21:20bβ-22) and the following verses (21:23-26) braid together at least three narratorial voices. Elijah's speech is commandeered by a first narrative voice that shifts the grounds of Ahab's condemnation from Naboth's murder to the sin of Jeroboam and introduces the idea of the obliteration of the guilty party's whole lineage. That same voice speaks even more strongly in 21:24. The narrator that accuses Ahab of unspecified "evil" in 21:25a is probably the same voice, since it repeats the idiom "sold himself to do evil" from verse 20bβ.[50] The other two narratorial voices take advantage of the first voice's inexplicit language ("evil") to introduce their own respective agendas. The voice in 21:26 identifies the "evil" of v. 25a as the worship of the *gillulîm* of the Amorites and includes a subtle reminder of the crime against Naboth, which the narrative voice of the earlier verses passed over in silence. Finally, there is a narrative voice that tries to deflect primary blame from Ahab to Jezebel (vv. 23 and 25b).[51] This last voice is aware of the others— it models Jezebel's punishment in v. 23 on that of Ahab's line in v. 24 and

---

[50] The accusation of unparalleled "evil" is also connected with following the way of Jeroboam in 16:25-26 (said of Omri). In Ahab's case two accusations of unparalleled evil (16:30 and 33) surround specific charges that he both followed the way of Jeroboam *and* introduced the cult of Baal to Samaria.

[51] Note the rhetorical ploys this narrator uses. The general accusation of unspecified "evil" refers to the sin of Jeroboam; this is clear from the parallels to 16:25-26, 30, 33 mentioned in the preceding note, and from the echo of "sold himself to do evil" in 21:20b, where the phrase introduced the citations of the condemnations of Jeroboam and Baasha. Yet Jezebel, worshiper of Baal, certainly had nothing to do with promoting the calf sanctuaries at Dan and Bethel! Because the "evil" in 21:25a is not made explicit, the narrative voice of 21:25b can co-opt it for the condemnation of Jezebel and imply that the "evil" in view is the judicial murder of Naboth that she engineered. There is also a bit of narratorial obfuscation involved. Jezebel is condemned for "urging Ahab to evil"; yet on any reading of 21:1-16 it is Jezebel who perpetrates the evil and, if anything, it is Ahab who urges her to it.

presents its remarks as elaborations of the other narrators' words.[52] The other voices, however, show no awareness of the anti-Jezebel "corrections" of this last voice.

The narrator tells us of Ahab's behavior "when he heard these words." Since Elijah's words to Ahab say nothing explicit about Naboth's murder, it is not clear whether Ahab's acts express penitence for his crime or mourning for himself and his doomed descendants. Since the encounter between Elijah and Ahab takes place in the vineyard he has seized, the king may well draw the connection; but if he does, the narrator gives us no clear indication of it. Finally, YHWH speaks again, approving Ahab's submission.

The second set of questions asks whether the interweaving of voices in 21:17-29 can help clarify the ambiguity we saw in the portrayal of Ahab in 21:1-16. That ambiguity offered two alternatives: that Ahab was a weak monarch, with Jezebel the devious power behind the throne, or that Ahab was a cunning and manipulative king who used Jezebel as a tool to get what he wanted. In the former case Jezebel would be the main culprit; in the latter, Ahab would be. In 21:17-29 most of the voices we hear are unanimous in their focus on Ahab as the guilty party. YHWH's condemnation not only targets Ahab and passes over Jezebel in silence; it also echoes Jezebel's imperatives in 21:15 (see above, p. 54) to counterpose Ahab and Elijah as principal and opposing figures. Elijah likens him to kings whose deeds brought disaster on their houses, but does not mention Jezebel. One narratorial voice speaks of him in terms of unparalleled evil (21:25a), another in terms of idolatry. In 21:17-29 only one narrative voice—that heard in 21:23 and 21:25b—attempts to identify Jezebel as the principal evil figure. The different points of view espoused by the various voices confirm that the alternative portrayals we discerned in 21:1-16 were both valid and reasonable readings of the story. But the preponderance of voices here in favor of seeing Ahab as the focus of evil, along with the recognition that the anti-Jezebel voice "corrects" the others, gives the anti-Jezebel point of view the feel of revisionist history.

Finally, is it possible to hear, in this bewildering chorus of voices, a single overarching meaning? To answer this question we need to look more closely at a couple of elements in the chapter that do not fit smoothly into their narrative context; rather, they seem extraneous to both the plot and the agendas of the main narrative voices we have noted. We will see that these elements point in a direction that adds an entire new level of meaning

---

[52] Note how the "also" that begins v. 23 presumes the context of guilt and punishment supplied by v. 22. Similarly, the anti-Jezebel words of v. 25b ("urged on by his wife Jezebel") presume the preceding main clause that they qualify.

to the story. The first element is the phrase "who [is] in Samaria" in 21:18. As we saw above, this harks back to the rare title "King of Samaria" in 21:1 and together those usages evoke the anti-Baalist theme of 1 Kings 17–19. The second element is the unprecedented charge in 21:26 that Ahab went after *gillulîm*, "as the Amorites had done, whom the LORD drove out [dispossessed; *yāraš*] before the Israelites." The juxtaposition of the themes of idolatry and taking possession invites us to explore the possibility of a connection between Ahab's Baalism and his taking possession *(yāraš)* of Naboth's patrimony. As background for this exploration it is important to remember that "YHWH's vineyard" is a commonly used symbol for Israel in the Hebrew Bible (see, for instance, Isa 3:14; 5:1-7; Jer 12:10), and that 1 Kings envisages Baal as a foreign deity introduced into Israel from outside by Jezebel and Ahab (see n. 14, ch. 1 above). These observations suggest that on a deep level the usurpation of Naboth's vineyard by Ahab and Jezebel is emblematic of the attempted usurpation of YHWH's vineyard by the god Baal, whose worship both Ahab and Jezebel promoted. Once, YHWH dispossessed "the (gods of the) Amorites" to give his people the land of Israel; now Ahab and Jezebel are striving to dispossess YHWH of the patrimony he has given to Israel and hand it over to a new deity from without, Baal. The crime against Naboth stands for this crime against YHWH and incurs dynastic disaster as punishment not only because it is sacrilegious abuse of legal and religious practice, as well as murder, but also because it represents the far more heinous evil of direct attack on YHWH's status as the God of Israel.

Chapter 22: Ahab and the Aramean Wars: Ahab's Defeat and Death

The last chapter of the Ahab story returns to the international stage and the hostilities between Aram and Israel that were the focus of chapter 20. As in the earlier chapter, there are two narrative voices, one admiring of Ahab and the other condemnatory. In chapter 22, however, the negative voice intervenes very early in the chapter and its contribution is substantially longer than the surrounding story. Its condemnation of Ahab shapes the way the reader receives the rest of the story. In this way it preempts and obscures what would otherwise be a positive presentation of the king. We will look first at the story told by the positive narrative voice (22:1-4, 29-36), then at the transformation of that story by the negative narrative voice (22:5-28). Finally, we will consider the concluding verses of the whole Ahab story, 22:37-40.

22:1-4, 29-36

It has been three years since the peace treaty between Ben-hadad and Ahab (20:34),[53] and Israel's situation has changed considerably. Ahab is much stronger than he was. Whereas in chapter 20 he was vassal to Ben-hadad, he now seems to be overlord to Jehoshaphat of Judah.[54] He is, in fact, so strong that he contemplates a military offensive against Aram, based on the claim that Ben-hadad has not kept one of the terms of the earlier treaty. He had promised, "I will restore the towns that my father took from your father" (20:34); Ahab asserts, to the contrary, that "Ramoth Gilead belongs to us, yet we are doing nothing to take it out of the hand of the king of Aram" (22:3). The tables are thus turned: Ahab, not Ben-hadad, is the aggressor; Ahab, not Ben-hadad, has a royal vassal as an ally (Ben-hadad had had "thirty-two kings" among his forces: 20:1). Jehoshaphat pledges himself to the war effort.[55]

After the prophetic story told by the negative narrative voice (22:5-28), to which we will return, the positive voice continues with the immediate preparations for battle (22:29-30). Ahab orders Jehoshaphat to wear his regalia while Ahab himself dons ordinary battle gear.[56] Under normal circumstances a king would remain at the back of his army, in the most protected position, as visible symbol and practical rallying point for his troops. Ahab's idea is to put Jehoshaphat in that position and thus free himself to dress as an ordinary soldier and go into the thick of the battle. The narrator confirms that this is what he does. Considered in itself, this deed presents Ahab in a positive light. It highlights his courage and willingness to risk himself, and his readiness to offer protection to his vassal.

---

[53] Note that in 1 Kings 22 the king of Israel is named as Ahab only in 22:20, and the king of Aram is never named. This anonymity will be significant for the redactional analysis later in our study, which will argue that the stories of the Aramean war have been transferred to Ahab from the reign of some later Israelite king. In the present narrative context, however, the kings are clearly to be understood as the Ahab and Ben-hadad of chapter 20.

[54] Although the text does not say so in so many words, the considerable parallels between the relationship of Ahab to Ben-hadad in chapter 20 and the relationship of Jehoshaphat to Ahab in chapter 22 are decisive. Ahab's submissive words in 20:4 parallel Jehoshaphat's in 22:4; Ahab calls Ben-hadad "my lord the king" (20:4, 9); Jehoshaphat calls Ahab "the king" (22:8). The wording of 22:1-2 suggests that Jehoshaphat of Judah is to be numbered among the "servants" whom Ahab of Israel consults about his plans for war.

[55] Jehoshaphat's language is terse and untranslatable: "Like me, like you; like my people, like your people; like my horses, like your horses." Thus he pledges not only chariotry and army (this is the meaning of "people"; see n. 12 above); he also promises to take part personally in the battle along with Ahab.

[56] The Hebrew text is difficult here. This reading follows the general consensus among scholars.

The battle itself (22:31-33) mentions Ahab only in passing, in the words of the king of Aram. He enjoins his allies to center their attack on the king of Israel. It is not clear whether this is simply good strategy (killing the king would demoralize the Israelite army) or personal vendetta based, presumably, on Ben-hadad's view that Ahab's attack represents a violation of their treaty. We learn nothing particularly insightful about Ahab from the fact that his enemy and former overlord wishes him dead. There is an ironic nuance to the scene, however. Ahab's ploy of disguising himself so that he could brave the dangers of battle in fact serves to protect him from Ben-hadad's assault.

Ahab's death is the focus of 22:34-36, and it is recorded in minute and graphic detail. An anonymous soldier fatally wounds him. The text simply describes the bowman as "somebody," and it says that he drew his bow "in wholeness." That term is unclear in this context. It can refer to physical strength ("to his full strength") and explain why the arrow he loosed was able to pierce the king's armor. Most interpreters, however, take it in its more common moral sense ("innocence, integrity") and understand it as meaning that the soldier was not aware of his target's identity. In other words, the attack is not aimed at Ahab in obedience to Ben-hadad's order in 22:31, but is merely one of those random blows of which pitched battles are made. Ahab's death is the tragic result of his courageous willingness to risk himself in battle. And thus the ironies pile up: If Ahab's willingness to eschew the safety of the king's position results, paradoxically, in saving him from Ben-hadad, his courage in entering into the dangers of battle proves rash when he becomes a random casualty of war.

Ahab does not die immediately. His words to his chariot driver are understandable, given the seriousness of Ahab's wound,[57] but the chariot is hemmed in and cannot withdraw from the battle. Ahab is forced by the press to remain while his lifeblood drains away. Here the narrator is making a further ironic comment on Ahab's misguided strategy of disguise. The king who pretended to be a soldier in order to be able to enter the battle now cannot escape the battle and, as a result, becomes a corpse "propped up in his chariot facing the Arameans," pretending not to be dead. The call for retreat (22:36) suggests that there was no victory for Israel, but it is not clear that there was a defeat either. The narrator seems less interested in the outcome of the battle than in the tragic death of a brave but foolhardy king.

[57] There is one oddity in the words that should not be pressed too far. In Hebrew, Ahab says "carry me out of the *camp*," not "out of the *battle*"; most English versions follow the ancient Greek translation, which reads "carry me out of the battle." The two phrases are rather similar in Hebrew consonantal writing (*mnhmhnh*, "out of the camp"; *mnhmlhmh*, "out of the battle") and may have been confused by a scribe in the process of copying a manuscript.

22:5-28

Yet the tragic story of a noble but reckless king is not what most readers find in this chapter. The reason is the lengthy scene of prophetic condemnation in 22:5-28; it expresses a negative view of Ahab that transforms the meaning of everything that follows to fit its own agenda. We will look first at the passage itself, then consider how it radically alters the way we read the rest of the story.

The tale of prophetic condemnation begins with Jehoshaphat, Ahab's Judean vassal, who proposes that before undertaking a military campaign his overlord ought to consult the will of YHWH as communicated through a prophet. Without further comment Ahab assembles four hundred prophets. The phenomenon of group prophecy is attested elsewhere in the Bible, both among non-Israelite prophets (e.g., the "four hundred fifty prophets of Baal" on Mount Carmel, 18:20-29) and among Israelite prophets (1 Sam 10:5-6). It must be noted, however, that despite Jehoshaphat's specific request to inquire "of the LORD"[58] the narrator does not describe the prophets whom Ahab assembles as prophets of any particular deity.[59] Ahab's question to the prophets is straightforward. He wants to know whether his campaign against Ramoth Gilead is in accord with the divine will or not.

The prophets' answer does not identify them as prophets of YHWH, despite the wording of the *NRSV*. To understand why, we must take a bit of a detour and look briefly at a fairly technical aspect of biblical studies called "textual criticism."

---

[58] The Hebrew Bible uses several different words to refer to God. One, *'dny* (pronounced *'ădōnî* or *'ădōnāy*), means "Lord," and is translated that way in English Bibles. It can be used of anyone, human or divine, whom one acknowledges as one's "lord." Another, *yhwh* (pronunciation uncertain, but probably *yahweh*) is the personal name of Israel's deity, and was traditionally not spoken; instead, one reading the biblical text would substitute *'ădōnāy* or some other term. Most English Bibles follow this tradition, and use the term "LORD" (or sometimes "GOD") where the Hebrew has *yhwh*. However, English Bibles generally indicate typographically which term is in the Hebrew text by using small capital letters (LORD or GOD) for *yhwh* and ordinary lower case (Lord) for *'ădōnāy*. In 1 Kings 22:5 Jehoshaphat asks to inquire specifically "of YHWH."

[59] In the larger context the picture is complicated by Elijah's claim some time earlier to be the only remaining prophet of YHWH (18:22; see also 19:10, 14). It is intriguing to speculate on the fact that Ahab assembles *four hundred* prophets for his oracle. In 1 Kings 18 Elijah ordered Ahab to gather the "four hundred prophets of Asherah" (Asherah was a popular Canaanite goddess) along with the prophets of Baal. Nothing further is said of the prophets of Asherah—neither whether Ahab actually gathered them nor whether Elijah killed them along with the prophets of Baal (18:40).

Excursus on Textual Criticism

All ancient writings were handwritten, of course. As need or occasion arose they would be copied, also by hand, and the copies would circulate and spawn further copies. Anyone who has ever tried to copy a lengthy document by hand knows how difficult it is to do so perfectly, without a single difference between original and copy. It is virtually impossible not to misspell something, or leave out something, or copy a word twice, etc., not to mention the constant temptation to "improve" the original. It should come as no surprise, therefore, to find a large number of differences among the ancient biblical manuscripts we possess. In theory all copies go back to a single original text. But in practice we no longer possess any of the originals; all we have are copies, and copies of copies—and these do not all agree. Is it possible to reconstruct the wording of the original that lies behind the variations in the copies? This is the goal of textual criticism.

It would take us too far afield to go into the technicalities of the method, but the basic principle that textual criticism applies to choose between variant readings is worth considering. Given two ancient manuscripts, one with "Reading A" and the other with "Reading B," there are two possible ways to understand the difference. Either "Reading A" is original and "Reading B" is secondary, or "Reading B" is original and "Reading A" is secondary. The textual critic asks the same question of each possibility: What process could cause the secondary reading to arise from the original reading? Then the critic compares the two answers, and judges which process is more likely to have occurred. To give a simple example, if both readings mean substantially the same thing, but one is grammatically or stylistically better than the other, then is it more likely that a copyist improved the language or made it worse? Clearly, when a copyist, instead of reproducing the text as it is, chooses to change it for purely stylistic or grammatical reasons, he or she will be more likely to *improve* the text. And so the stylistically superior text is probably secondary, and the less polished reading is more likely original.

The present text gives us a good opportunity to see textual criticism in action. In 22:6 the prophets reply to Ahab's request for an oracle. In some of our ancient Hebrew manuscripts they say, "Go up, so that the lord may give into the king's hand." Other manuscripts say,

"Go up, so that YHWH may give into the king's hand." The challenge for a textual critic is to determine whether "lord" is original and a copyist secondarily changed it to "YHWH," or vice versa.

Many scholars deem that "YHWH" is original here.[60] They reason that, since the prophets are prophesying a falsehood (Ahab will not in fact survive the battle), they are false prophets; one copyist was uncomfortable having false prophets prophesy with the sacrosanct divine name, and so in his manuscript he replaced "YHWH" with the less sacred term "lord." Manuscripts that read "lord" are copies descended from his; manuscripts that read "YHWH" reflect the original. However, there are objections to this reasoning. It does not explain, for instance, why that copyist allowed the name "YHWH" to remain in the same prophets' mouths at 22:11 and 12. (There are no manuscript variants at those points; all sources agree that "YHWH" belongs there.) Other scholars reason in the opposite direction: The original text of 22:6 read "lord" and a later copyist changed it in 22:6 to match the "YHWH" in 22:12, since it is the same prophets uttering the same oracle in both places. This opinion will serve as the basis for our reading, and we shall treat "lord" as the original reading.

A textual critical decision on this point is unavoidable; we must read the text one way or the other. And in the last analysis our decision comes down to a judgment call. Yet it has considerable impact on how we read the first part of this passage. If the four hundred prophets use the name "YHWH," their allegiance is clarified and Ahab is seen to have complied with Jehoshaphat's request. If the four hundred prophets use the term "lord," their allegiance is not clear and there is a real possibility that Ahab is attempting to mislead Jehoshaphat and avoid contact with YHWH prophets.[61]

---

[60] The *NRSV*'s "LORD" follows this opinion. See n. 58 for the explanation of the difference between "LORD" and "lord."

[61] Other ambiguities in the prophets' words should also be noted. In 22:6 they do not say, as the *NRSV* translates, "for the LORD will give"; the Hebrew verb form could mean "so that the Lord may give," or "and may the Lord give," but it cannot be translated as a straightforward promise. Further, the king to whom the "lord" will award victory is unnamed. Ahab will assume that it is he, but the prophetic oracle does not say so. The oracle has a Delphic quality that allows the hearer to interpret it almost any way he or she wishes. When the prophets repeat their oracle in 22:12 it will no longer be ambiguous.

Jehoshaphat's comment does not clarify the issue. He asks Ahab, "Is there not still a prophet of YHWH . . . ?" (The *NRSV*'s "no other prophet of the LORD" implies that the four hundred prophets were also prophets of YHWH, but the Hebrew does not require such an understanding.) Ahab grudgingly concedes that there is, one Micaiah, son of Imlah,[62] and explains why Ahab is loath to consult him. When Jehoshaphat's reply is polite but unyielding, Ahab summons Micaiah.

The narrative now indulges in a bit of delay. While the messenger goes off to find Micaiah we are treated to a description of the scene, and to a repetition of the four hundred prophets' oracle. Both involve subtle characterizations of Ahab. First of all, scenic description is extremely rare in biblical Hebrew narrative; when it occurs it is usually fraught with implications. Here the two kings are enthroned in a formal gathering place (the "threshing floor at the entrance of the gate" would be the largest open space in the town, and therefore a place of formal public assembly), surrounded by their courtiers and the four hundred prophets. This solemn picture establishes the first pole of an ironic contrast; the opposite pole will be Micaiah's description of a scene in heaven's royal court (22:19-23); we will examine this contrast in greater detail below.

Second, the four hundred prophets repeat their oracle, but with a few telling differences. First, their apparent leader, Zedekiah ben Kenaanah, performs a symbolic action for which he invokes YHWH's name. (Prophetic actions like this are commonly used by both true and false prophets in the Hebrew Bible; they seem to have been conventional modes of prophetic expression.) Then the four hundred prophets restate their promise of success to Ahab, this time explicitly invoking YHWH's name.[63] The prophets' willingness to present their oracle in YHWH's name tells us much about them, and implies much about Ahab as well. When they were first summoned to the kings' presence Ahab asked them for an oracle, but did not specify what deity they were to consult. In their response the prophets simply spoke in the name of "the lord." Now, however, they have heard Jehoshaphat explicitly request an oracle in YHWH's name (22:7), and they have heard Ahab send for a known prophet of YHWH. They revise their oracle accordingly. In

---

[62] In the larger context of 1 Kings 17–19 the reader expects Ahab to name Elijah as the prophet he hates. When he names an otherwise unknown Micaiah ben Imlah we are reminded of the anonymous prophet who condemned Ahab in 20:35-43 and we surmise that Ahab's problems with prophets were not limited to one or two fanatical opponents.

[63] They also resolve the other ambiguities in their original oracle (see n. 61). By inserting the imperative verb "triumph" they make the oracle a clear promise of victory to the hearer, Ahab. Further, they avoid the verb form that means "so that YHWH may give" and use an explicitly future form, "and YHWH will give."

other words, they are sycophants, willing to speak whatever they think the king wants to hear. But that implies—and we will see confirmation of this in a moment—that they perceive Ahab as the sort of king who wants yes-men around him, not people who will stand up to him.

Meanwhile, the messenger has reached Micaiah ben Imlah, and explains the situation to him. He urges Micaiah to tell the king what he wants to hear (22:13), just as the other prophets are doing. In other words, it is not only sycophants who perceive Ahab this way, but even Ahab's court staff. Micaiah's refusal of the messenger's advice forewarns the reader of the imminent conflict between Micaiah and the other prophets, but not of the surprising twists that conflict will take. When Micaiah reaches the kings, Ahab poses the same question. There is one significant difference between Ahab's words in 22:6 and those in 22:15. To the four hundred prophets Ahab spoke only of himself ("Shall *I* go up . . . or shall *I* refrain?"); to Micaiah he includes Jehoshaphat in his question ("Shall *we* go . . . or shall *we* refrain?"). Since Ahab believes that Micaiah "never prophesies anything favorable about" Ahab (22:8), his inclusion of Jehoshaphat in the oracle is most probably an attempt to supply Micaiah with a reason to prophesy something favorable.

The story suddenly becomes bewildering. Micaiah, who pledged to say whatever YHWH commanded him to say, says exactly the same thing as the four hundred prophets! And Ahab, who earlier complained that Micaiah "never prophesies anything favorable about me," rejects Micaiah's favorable oracle as untrue, even though it agrees with what his four hundred prophets have said! How can we make sense of this behavior, which seems out of character for both prophet and king? Paradoxically, the best way to understand it is to take it straight. Micaiah pledged to say whatever YHWH told him to say. Therefore this oracle is what YHWH gave him to say, and it confirms that the oracle of the four hundred prophets is inspired by YHWH. (The obvious difficulty with this interpretation, of course, is that the oracle will not come true. We will see the reason for this in a moment.) Ahab, in turn, is so taken aback by the fact that Micaiah prophesied favorably for him that he immediately doubts Micaiah (and by implication he doubts the four hundred prophets with whom Micaiah is in agreement). He adjures Micaiah to tell the truth not, perhaps, because he is really interested in YHWH's wishes, but because Micaiah's positive oracle contradicts his claim to Jehoshaphat about the prophet's unrelenting disapproval. In reply, Micaiah prophesies Ahab's death.[64] Ahab's comment to Jehoshaphat says, in effect, "I told you so!"

---

[64] "Shepherd" is a common metaphor for the king in ancient Near Eastern cultures. Micaiah's vision of Israel "scattered on the mountains, like sheep that have no shepherd," and the confirming divine word that "these have no master," in effect announce that the king is going to be lost.

Micaiah is not finished, however. He goes on to describe a vision he had of the royal court of YHWH (22:19-23). Despite the *NRSV*'s introduction, "Therefore hear the word of the LORD,"[65] what follows is not an oracle spoken in God's name but an account by Micaiah of deliberations he witnessed in the divine council in heaven. He begins by describing the scene (22:19). This is the second part of the ironic contrast with the description of the two kings, enthroned and arrayed in their regalia, surrounded by the four hundred prophets (22:10). The contrast is sardonic. While the two kings sit resplendently robed, surrounded by fawning yes-men, thinking that they are making great decisions, the true power in the universe is enthroned above them, surrounded by his advisers, deciding their fate.

Micaiah reveals that YHWH has laid a trap for Ahab by inspiring his prophets to lie to him about the outcome of his campaign against Ramoth Gilead. In other words, the oracle of the four hundred prophets and Micaiah's oracle in agreement with theirs (22:15b) *are* divinely inspired. The falsehood lies not in the prophets but in the divine spirit that inspires them.[66] YHWH's approval of the spirit's plan, Micaiah explains, is because

[65] The command "Hear the word of YHWH" is sometimes used as a "messenger formula" to introduce a divine oracle, usually in combination with the more common messenger formula "Thus says YHWH." In 22:19a, however, it does not introduce an oracle given as YHWH's words, where "I" would mean YHWH, but a narrative where "I" is Micaiah himself. The Hebrew word *dābār* has a much broader meaning than just "word"; it can also mean a whole story, or a non-verbal "matter" or "issue." (Compare the English question from one friend to another about an absent third, "Is there any word of George?") So Micaiah's words here can just as correctly be translated, "Hear this story about YHWH."

[66] Needless to say, most readers find this a very uncomfortable passage. How can God engage in deception? The depth of theological unease Micaiah's vision provokes in modern scholars can be measured by the enormous literature that has tried to tackle the question. See, for example, J. J. M. Roberts, "Does God Lie? Divine Deceit as a Theological Problem in Israelite Prophetic Literature," in John A. Emerton, ed., *Congress Volume: Jerusalem 1986*, VTSup 40 (Leiden: Brill, 1988) 211–20; Jeffries M. Hamilton, "Caught in the Nets of Prophecy," *Catholic Biblical Quarterly* 56 (1994) 649–63; and most recently Robert B. Chisholm, Jr., "Does God Deceive?" *Bibliotheca Sacra* 155 (1998) 12–28. For a survey of older discussions of the whole chapter see Wolfgang Roth, "The Story of the Prophet Micaiah (1 Kings 22) in Historical-Critical Interpretation 1876–1976," in Robert M. Polzin and Eugene Rothman, eds., *The Biblical Mosaic: Changing Perspectives*. Semeia Studies (Philadelphia: Fortress; Chico: Scholars Press, 1982) 105–37. It is useful here to recall some of the concepts and categories of narrative criticism. "God" or "YHWH" in 1 Kings 22 is *a character,* and characters in narratives are creations of the author. They are built out of words. Even when the character bears the same name as someone who exists in the real world, the author is not obliged to construct someone who is identical in all respects. And so the text's "Moses" or "David"—or "God"—need not portray the Moses or David of history, or the God we worship, with absolute accuracy. Granted, it is a provocative act on the part of the author to present a "YHWH" who lies, but its challenge need not be understood as blasphemy.

YHWH "has decreed disaster for you."⁶⁷ We learn from this scene that, according to Micaiah, YHWH is set on Ahab's destruction. However, we have only Micaiah's word for that, and the narrator offers no independent confirmation of it. Ahab is in a similar situation: He hears Micaiah's claims but has no means to verify or falsify them. As readers we can wait to see how things turn out; Ahab is not so privileged: He has to act on the information he has.

Zedekiah ben Kenaanah, leader and spokesman of the four hundred prophets, assaults Micaiah physically and verbally (22:24). His words and Micaiah's reply add nothing to the characterization of Ahab, but one clever double meaning is worth noting. When Zedekiah asks, "Which way did the spirit of the Lord pass from me to speak to you?" he is not simply challenging Micaiah's claim to be a prophet. He is alluding to Micaiah's assertion that the spirit of the four hundred prophets is a "lying spirit," and implying thereby that Micaiah's claims about the heavenly court and the divine plot are the real lies that Ahab is being told.

Finally Ahab orders Micaiah imprisoned, "until I come in peace"⁶⁸ (22:27). This is neither vindictiveness nor bravado. It does not mean that Ahab believes Micaiah but is going to go his own way anyway. It means that he does *not* believe Micaiah, but will not be able to prove that Micaiah is a false prophet until he, Ahab, comes home safely from the war. Until that time Micaiah is to be kept in custody, so that he can then be tried (and executed—see Deut 18:20) for false prophecy. Ahab's sin is not only disobedience to YHWH's word but also dismissal of it as a divine word in the first place.

Let us summarize our discussion of 22:5-28. The scene of prophetic condemnation is the utterance of a narrative voice whose attitudes to Ahab are entirely negative. It depicts him as reluctant to involve himself with YHWH or his prophet. When Ahab is compelled to deal with a prophet of

---

It may simply be a shocking means to convey a theological message most forcefully. Here, for instance, the narrator's claim is that God's will is inescapable, no matter how cleverly Ahab attempts to circumvent it. In fact, when Micaiah reveals YHWH's plan to Ahab, his announcement of the *děbar yhwh* (the "story about YHWH," but also the "word of YHWH") allows Ahab the opportunity to see through the lying spirit's deception. Ahab fails—or perhaps refuses—to do so.

⁶⁷ Literally "YHWH has spoken evil against you." The alert reader will hear the echo in this "evil" of the words of Elijah in 21:21. The *NRSV* preserves the echo by translating the word "disaster" in both places.

⁶⁸ "Peace" is not really the best translation for *šālôm* here. The Hebrew word means "wholeness," that is, "everything is the way it should be." Since Ahab is speaking of returning from battle, he means here "until I come back victorious."

YHWH, he is dismissive of the prophet's warning. No specific charges are laid to Ahab's account in the chapter; nevertheless, YHWH actively seeks his destruction. This narrator is quite different from the one we heard speaking as we read 22:1-4, 29-38, and his negative presentation inevitably colors the way a reader encounters what follows it. We must *re-read* vv. 29-36 to appreciate the negative narrator's genius.

Immediately after the prophetic condemnation of Ahab the story turns to the kings' preparations for battle: Jehoshaphat dons his royal robes and takes the battlefield position of the king, visible but safe; Ahab wears ordinary soldier's armor and goes into the front lines. Without the intervening scene of prophetic condemnation, we saw that this action portrayed Ahab as brave but foolhardy—brave, because he gave up safety to risk the dangers of combat; foolhardy because, as things turned out, he was fatally wounded. However, once a reader has heard the negative narratorial voice's story, in which Ahab is warned by Micaiah of YHWH's plot, the exchange of clothing takes on a totally different meaning. Instead of an act of bravery it becomes an act of cowardice; instead of foolhardiness Ahab exhibits cunning. He may not believe Micaiah, but he does not hesitate to hedge his bets. If YHWH intends to use the hazards of battle to compass Ahab's death, Ahab will use Jehoshaphat as a decoy to draw YHWH's stroke.

It doesn't work, of course. The blow falls anyway: A random soldier "drew his bow and unknowingly struck the king of Israel." Without the intervening negative voice we would read this as the tragic result of Ahab's recklessness in entering the fray, but after the scene of prophetic condemnation we cannot help but see this arrow as divinely guided. No mere masquerade is enough to enable Ahab's escape from YHWH's sight. Likewise the press that hems Ahab's chariot in and leaves him to bleed to death on the field of battle takes on the aura of divine machination. Finally, the cry to retreat that sounds in 22:36 now resounds as a fulfillment of Micaiah's vision in 22:17b: "And the LORD said, 'These have no master; let each one go home in peace.'"

The pattern of 22:1-36, then, resembles that of chapter 20. There are two narrative voices, one positive and one negative, that tell us of Ahab's wars with Aram. The positive voice portrays the king in admirable terms; the negative voice is strongly condemnatory. Further, in each chapter the negative voice seems aware of the positive voice, though the converse is not true. In chapter 22 there is one indication of this awareness. The negative narrator's reference to the kings' regalia in 22:10 ("arrayed in their robes") plays no part in his later satirical contrast between the earthly and heavenly throne scenes, since there is no comparable description of

YHWH's raiment in 22:19. Its only function is to introduce the motif of royal clothing, which belongs to the positive narrator's tale otherwise, and so to foreshadow the ironic role that royal clothing and disguise will play in the battle itself.

22:37-40

This is not the end of the story, however. How do the last four verses fit into this dialogue of two voices? And is there, as there was in chapter 20, any way to discern behind this dialogue the unified and unifying vision of the author? Verse 37 is the natural conclusion to the positive narrator's story of Ahab's death in 22:29-36. But it contains a last subtle irony against Ahab that may indicate an infiltration of the positive narrator's speech by the negative narrator. The king has had Micaiah imprisoned "until I come in peace" (i.e., safe and victorious; 22:27). The narrator tells us in 22:37 that "the king died *and came to Samaria*" (the *NRSV* obscures the irony by translating "and *was brought* to Samaria"). As he anticipated, Ahab "came" back to Samaria; what he did not anticipate was being dead when he did so! The remark completes the pervasive motif of disguise that began with the kings exchanging robes, reached its climax with the corpse of Ahab propped up in his chariot "facing the Arameans" as if he were not *hors de combat,* and culminates here with the grotesque image of the dead king actively "coming" to Samaria for burial. On the other hand, 22:38 comes entirely from the negative narrative voice. The remark about washing Ahab's blood from his chariot presupposes 22:35; conversely, the remark in 22:35 about the blood from Ahab's wound pooling in the bottom of the chariot has no other purpose than to prepare for 22:38.[69] At the same time, 22:38 points outside the story to an oracle reminiscent of, though not identical with, Elijah's words in 21:19.[70] In this way the negative narrator hints that the prophetic opposition to Ahab represented by this narrative voice is much more widespread than we realize.

---

[69] This is a rather technical point, but the Hebrew does not say, as the *NRSV* translates it, that "the blood *had flowed* into the bottom of the chariot," as if it were describing Ahab bleeding to death. The Hebrew says, ". . . at evening he died; and [then] the blood of the wound flowed into the bottom of the chariot." The verb form used conveys the meaning that the flowing of the blood *followed* the dying.

[70] The similarity, of course, is the image of dogs licking up Ahab's blood. The differences, however, include that Elijah foretold that this would happen in Jezreel ("the same place"; compare 21:19 and 21:13), whereas in 22:38 it happens "by the pool of Samaria"; and there is no mention of prostitutes bathing in Ahab's blood in Elijah's oracle.

The story of Ahab ends with the same sort of formulaic conclusion that concludes almost every king's reign from 1 Kings 11:41-43 to the end of 2 Kings (1 Kgs 22:39-40). There is nothing specifically positive or negative implied about Ahab in these verses, though the mention of Ahab's "ivory house" may have had resonances for the ancient audience that we no longer perceive.[71] There is one indication that this narrative voice is the least aware of all those we have encountered, though that indication will only be noticed by someone extremely familiar with the two books of Kings. The phrase "slept with his ancestors," as a euphemism for death, occurs very frequently in the concluding formulas for a king's reign. However, it never occurs when the king has died by violence.[72] This means that the voice that speaks in 22:40 knows neither the story of Ahab's death in battle nor the one of the prophetic condemnation that foreshadowed it.

As in 1 Kings 20, the tension between positive and negative narrative voices is not balanced. The positive voice is subordinated to the negative, and the latter fundamentally constrains the reader's understanding of the positive voice's narrative. In 1 Kings 20 the negative narrator waited until the positive narrator had his say, then stepped in to add a new, negative interpretation to what had gone before. In 1 Kings 22, however, the negative narrator enters as early as v. 5. His story of prophetic condemnation precludes any positive understanding of Ahab's subsequent behavior. In this way the ironic twist that transforms the royal disguise from bravery to cowardice and the random arrow from tragic mishap to divine strike does not *add* a new meaning but *suppresses and replaces* the positive meaning that could otherwise have been perceived. The unified and unifying meaning, then, lies much closer to the negative narrator's vision here than in 1 Kings 20.

---

[71] Is it, for instance, an allusion to the time of Ahab as a time of impressive and beautiful public buildings? Is it intended as a parallel to the building of Jericho, mentioned at the beginning of Ahab's reign (16:34), which cost the builder two of his sons? (Ahab's son and successor, Ahaziah, will die from a fall after a reign of only a year and a few months. He will be succeeded by another of Ahab's sons, Jehoram, who will eventually be assassinated.) Does the mention of "ivory" evoke exorbitant luxury, as we see in the prophecies of Amos (Amos 3:15; 6:4)?

[72] There is one possible exception to this pattern, but it does not occur in the stereotyped concluding formula to a regnal account. Second Kings 14:22 says that King Azariah restored Elath to Judah "after the king slept with his ancestors." ("The king" is not named in the Hebrew text, despite the *NRSV*'s insertion of "Amaziah.") If "the king" refers to Azariah's father, Amaziah, then this verse is an exception, since Amaziah was assassinated (2 Kgs 14:17-20). It is not clear, however, whether the reference is to Amaziah or to some other king, e.g., Jehoash of Israel (who died peacefully: 2 Kings 13:13), or perhaps the king of Edom who would have controlled Elath prior to Azariah's seizure of it.

Why, then, preserve elements of potentially positive import at all, if their positive potential is only going to be suppressed in favor of turning them to further blackening of Ahab's character? Why not simply present a story of Ahab that is clearly and thoroughly negative? The author's dilemma is oddly parallel to Micaiah's, and their respective strategies are similar as well. Like the four hundred prophets, Micaiah receives from the lying spirit the promise of Ahab's victory, and he proclaims it. Micaiah, though, knows that the promise's positive appearance is false. He demonstrates the deception by exposing the hidden truth of YHWH's ruse. Analogously, the author of our story possesses—presumably received from his traditional sources[73]—an admiring story of Ahab's bravery in battle. The author, however, is convinced that Ahab "did evil in the sight of the LORD more than all who were before him" (16:30) and that his death in battle, far from being a noble tragedy, was divine punishment for his egregious sins. And so the author positions his narrators' voices to *preserve,* but to completely *reinterpret,* the traditional story, and thereby to reveal Ahab's behavior as a cowardly attempt to escape YHWH's wrath rather than a courageous act of battlefield daring. There is an underlying cynicism in this chapter that was absent from 1 Kings 20. There the authorial vision acknowledged that there were positive and negative views of Ahab, even though it presented the negative views as more valid. Here the authorial vision insinuates that any positive view one may propose is simply a misreading of Ahab; even what might appear to be good qualities in him are ignobly motivated.

---

[73] It seems unlikely that an author so antipathetic to Ahab would have created out of whole cloth a story crediting Ahab with courage. It is more reasonable to assume that that story was already extant, and that the author was constrained to come to terms with it in some way. This sort of speculative attempt to reconstruct the history of the development of the story belongs more properly to the method called "redaction criticism," which we will explore in the next part of our study.

CONCLUSION

The Ahab of Narrative

Close reading has shown that the narrative presentation of Ahab in 1 Kings is complex in the extreme. In addition to the several views of the king that various characters in the narrative present (e.g., Elijah, Jezebel, YHWH), there are multiple narrators in these chapters, each of whom exhibits a unique perspective on him. The reader's first impression of Ahab is entirely negative—he "did evil . . . more than all who were before him" (16:30, 33). That impression will be nuanced as his character develops through the next six chapters, but it will never be wholly undone. Some narrative voices will describe the king positively, but whenever this occurs, another narrative voice will infiltrate the positive utterance to undermine or neutralize it. We have seen this in the complexities of chapters 20–22, but it is true as well even in the more straightforward characterizations of Ahab in chapters 17–19. In 18:5-6, for example, Ahab displays concern for livestock and a readiness to exert himself personally to save them. But the word "cut off" in his speech betrays the voice of a narrator who disparages Ahab by drawing the reader's attention to the contrast between his concern for animals and his willingness to allow Jezebel's destruction of prophets of YHWH (see above, p. 27). In 20:1-34 Ahab is a devout Yahwist, favored by God and obedient to God's prophets, prudent and even generous in his international negotiations. But a negative narrator adds vv. 35-43 and undercuts that positive impression by claiming that, at the end of the day, the voice of prophecy turned against Ahab and condemned his international dealings as disobedience to YHWH. In 22:1-38 the possibility of a positive reading of Ahab is precluded by an early narrative intervention that radically changes the valence of Ahab's actions from bravery to cowardice.

Elsewhere in the Ahab story negative portrayals of the king dominate, with no hint of positive appreciation. Elijah's confrontation with him in

18:17-19 is entirely hostile, as is Micaiah's in 22:5-28. Most stark is the story of Naboth's judicial murder in 1 Kings 21, whose ambiguity permits the reader to see Ahab either as a manipulated weakling or a devious manipulator, but in either case does not allow the slightest positive impression.

The negative voices, however, do not speak in unison about Ahab. He is condemned for infidelity to YHWH in several different forms: He continued the calf cults of Dan and Bethel (the "sins of Jeroboam," 16:31); he worshiped the "gods of the Amorites" (21:26); most heinous of all, he introduced the cult of Baal[1] into Israel and supported it (16:31-32). Ahab's Baalist proclivities also underlie the whole drama of chapters 17–19, and the awkward references to Samaria in 21:1 and 17 allude to them as well (see above, pp. 48, 54, and 64). Elsewhere he is portrayed as a follower of YHWH (20:1-34), though disobedient (20:35-43), or at least as recognizing the power of YHWH's prophet to speak truth (22:8, 16) even if he ignores what the prophet says. On the one hand Ahab is condemned as completely responsible for the evils of his day (16:30-33; 18:18; 20:42; 21:20-22, 25a, 26), and on the other as the pliant tool of his wicked and murderous wife (18:4; 19:1-2; 21:7, 8-10, 23, 25b).[2]

And so the ultimate question for the overall characterization of Ahab is the same one we have encountered several times already. Is there a unifying and unified vision of Ahab—an "authorial" viewpoint—that will do justice to the manifold voices in the text that each claim to present an authentic portrait? Clearly the overall impression of Ahab that a reader gets is negative. He was, in the last analysis, the "most evil" king the northern kingdom ever had. This is said of his father Omri first (16:25); when it is subsequently said of Ahab (16:30, 33), it means he surpassed his father in evil, presumably because of his introduction of the Baal cult into Israel (16:31-32). No other king of Israel, before or after, is so severely condemned. Yet the author does not suppress everything about Ahab that can nuance this condemnation. The very sketchy portrayal of Ahab in the Elijah stories (chapters 17–19) presents him as a committed Baalist, but Elijah's

---

[1] Related to the cult of Baal was the cult of the Canaanite goddess Asherah. It too is mentioned in the Ahab story, though only briefly. The reference to the "sacred pole" (16:33) is an allusion to the cult of Asherah, and Elijah asserts that alongside Ahab's four hundred fifty prophets of Baal he also has four hundred prophets of Asherah available (18:19), although they never actually appear in the story.

[2] Note how this motif, while clearly present in the texts, nevertheless appears in only a few, relatively limited passages. It is interesting (but beyond our scope in this work) to speculate how and why the diversion of responsibility from Israelite king to pagan queen became the principal lens through which much of our theological tradition has viewed the stories of Ahab.

invitation to renew the covenant (18:41) and the ambiguity of Ahab's response (see above, p. 31) leave room for the possibility of change. And indeed, when we reach the beginning of the stories that focus on Ahab himself, he appears to be an obedient and divinely favored devotee of YHWH. As a matter of fact, nowhere in chapters 20–22 is Ahab accused of overt Baalism. We must surmise that sometime between the years of drought and the end of Ahab's reign he was restored to YHWH's good graces, though the grounds for this restoration are never revealed to us.

The positive picture does not last, however. Each chapter of the Ahab stories contains a distinct prophetic condemnation of the king: by an unnamed prophet in 20:35-43, by Elijah in 21:17-29, and by Micaiah in 22:5-28. How do these various prophetic pronouncements comport with the "author's" viewpoint?

We have already seen indications that the author is not entirely in accord with the prophet's condemnation of Ahab for his treatment of Ben-hadad in chapter 20 (see above, p. 47). There are indications that the author has comparable reservations about YHWH's *forgiveness* of Ahab in chapter 21. Consider the contrasting parallels. In chapter 20, Ben-hadad, a foreign king, attacks Israel but is defeated. When he submits to Ahab, Ahab is magnanimous, and does not degrade him. Subsequently YHWH condemns Ahab for this compassion and insists that Ben-hadad should have been destroyed. In chapter 21 Naboth is an Israelite and a devout follower of YHWH; Ahab instigates his destruction. Then, when Ahab submits to YHWH, YHWH shows him compassion and exempts him from punishment. At the very least one can infer from this that, in the author's opinion, YHWH's reactions are inconsistent: If Ahab's compassion for Ben-hadad is blameworthy, how much more so Ahab's crime against Naboth?

Other elements in chapter 21 support this impression of the author's unease. First, the repetitiveness of the divine speech in 21:29, with its emphasis on how Ahab "has humbled himself before me," makes YHWH sound a bit smug; yet despite its wordiness the speech passes over in silence the underlying issue, namely, the unjust murder of Naboth and seizure of his property. It is as if, once Ahab has groveled, YHWH is satisfied; justice to the victim is no longer of concern. Second, there is a striking parallel between the two parts of chapter 21. In both *Ahab gets what he wants,* and in both he gets it by *fasting* (21:4-5, 27). If we read his first refusal to eat as a subtle manipulation of Jezebel, may we not suspect his fasting in response to Elijah's condemnation of being a way to manipulate YHWH? Finally, although there is no explicit accusation of Baalism in the chapter, the author's subtle allusions to Baalism (the references to Ahab as "king of/in Samaria") and to the usurpation of the "vineyard" (metaphorically, Israel as YHWH's vineyard) from its rightful owner insinuate that the royal couple's perversion of Israelite law and Yahwistic ritual is the moral equivalent of Baalism.

The author is suggesting, therefore, that Ahab's ostensive return to YHWH in chapter 20 was little more than a cosmetic makeover (foreshadowing, perhaps, the motif of "disguise" that develops in chapter 22?), and that his underlying values may be no less Baalist than they were in chapters 17–19.

In the prophetic condemnation in chapter 22, the divine decision to destroy the king once again converges with the author's judgment of Ahab's unmitigated evil. Ahab's continuing alienation from YHWH is hinted at in the ambiguous initial loyalties of the four hundred prophets he summons, in his reluctance to consult an avowed prophet of YHWH, and in the implication that beyond the stories of prophetic condemnations in chapters 17–22, others too had uttered "the word of YHWH" against Ahab (22:38). To the end Ahab remains identified with Samaria, his Baalist capital (22:37).

PART THREE
The Construction of the King

CHAPTER ONE

The Oldest Information

At this point in our study it is evident that there is a considerable gap between the Ahab we are able to reconstruct using historical methods and the Ahab who appears as a character in the narratives of 1 Kings. Is it possible to discern any continuity between the two? In other words, does the Ahab of the narratives have anything at all in common with the historical king for whom he is named? Might the narratives—despite the clearly partisan viewpoints of various narrators and presumed authors—contain retrievable historical data? And if they do, have the intermediate transmitters of those data altered in significant ways the information they received and handed on?

The reason we did not use the stories in 1 Kings 17–22 in our earlier historical reconstruction of King Ahab was the fact that they are not a contemporary or near-contemporary source of information. Most scholars agree that the Deuteronomic History (that is, the books of Joshua, Judges, 1–2 Samuel, and 1–2 Kings) is a single literary work dating, in its present form, no earlier than the mid-sixth century B.C.E. This situates it chronologically nearly three hundred years after the death of King Ahab; therefore it does not offer any contemporary or near-contemporary testimony to the king's reign. However, this is not the end of the road. There are indications that the Deuteronomic Historian had access to older records and used them in compiling his work.[1] We have already noted, for example, that the Deuteronomic History regularly names and recommends to its readers other sources of infor-

---

[1] Ancient literature was widely imitative of earlier writing. "Originality" does not seem to have been prized as it is today. Imitation was not slavish; it was a transformation—often profoundly creative—of what already existed. Nonetheless, it was imitation rather than an attempt to create something unprecedented. Consider, for instance, the transformation of Homer by Vergil, or, in the Semitic environment, the series of Deluge stories (Ziusudra,

mation (see n. 6 to Part One above), sources the Historian himself no doubt knew and used. It may be possible, then, to mine the Deuteronomic History for this older data, disentangle it from the later preoccupations of the Deuteronomist, and reconstruct some form of the earlier material. If that material can plausibly be dated to the ninth century B.C.E., it will bridge the chronological chasm and supply grist for the historical mill. At the same time, establishing, even conjecturally, some earlier stage of the traditions about Ahab will enable us to see more clearly how later transmitters such as the Deuteronomist modified those traditions in handing them on.

It will come as no surprise that the project of reconstructing the history of ancient Israel has been at the forefront of the agenda of critical biblical scholars from the first. Once it was recognized that the biblical texts are the end products of literary processes that lasted centuries, scholars realized that, to reconstruct the history of Israel, we must first reconstruct the history of the texts. To that end they developed several "historical critical" methods. Of particular interest for us are two of these methods, source criticism and redaction criticism. We will begin our study, as we did in Parts One and Two, with some discussion of the methods themselves before we undertake to apply those methods to the passages about Ahab.

We will also see, however, that there is a surprising overlap between historical criticism and narrative criticism. Both begin from observations about the text—often exactly the same observations—but offer alternative explanations. For example, what narrative criticism interprets as different narrative voices portraying different characterizations of Ahab and Jezebel, historical criticism may interpret as evidence for independent sources of information. And so, in a concluding reflection, we will take a moment to consider the implications of this overlap. Are we to understand these approaches as complementary or competing?

Historical Criticism

Source criticism

Source criticism attempts to discern where the author of the present text has drawn on earlier written sources and incorporated them. Further, it

<hr>

Atrahasis, Gilgamesh XI, Noah, Berossus). In the Hebrew Bible itself the reuse by 1–2 Chronicles of material from the books of Samuel and Kings shows that imitation can be at times almost verbatim, yet inspired by and expressive of a very different ideological outlook. On the practice of creative imitation in ancient literature see most recently Thomas L. Brodie, *The Birthing of the New Testament: The Intertextual Development of the New Testament Writings* (Sheffield: Sheffield Phoenix Press, 2004) 3–30.

attempts, insofar as possible, to identify what in the present text belonged to the earlier source and what represents the work of the later author. (This sort of author, whose authorship involves a great deal of free, creative editing of earlier materials, is called a "redactor." "Redaction criticism" then, as we shall see, will focus on the redactor's contribution; "source criticism" concentrates on the earlier written sources.) Finally, source criticism attempts to reconstruct, from the pieces that can be retrieved from the present text, the earlier written source.

The first step is identifying the presence of earlier source material in the present text. Suspicion begins with noticing a lack of coherence in the present text. Occasionally that incoherence will be obvious—e.g., a clear contradiction such as exists between Gen 6:19 and 7:2.[2] More often it will be more subtle: a difference in point of view, in implied values, in preferred vocabulary, in literary style, or the like. Such differences are less clear and, therefore, less conclusive. For instance, the hostility toward Jezebel evidenced in 1 Kings 21:23 and 25b is certainly different from the total blame placed on Ahab in vv. 25a and 26 of the same chapter, but are the two points of view so incompatible that we may (or must) think of independent sources? The argument gains in strength as it gains in weight: The more instances we find of anti-Jezebel passages with, say, characteristic vocabulary that never appears in passages that blame Ahab, and vice versa, the more likely the hypothesis that those two points of view have different origins. In the last analysis source criticism, no less than other analytical approaches, comes down to a judgment call.

The second step is to determine, as far as it is feasible, how the author of the present text (the "redactor") has modified the source document. Has the redactor added to or reworded the source? Has he omitted material or rearranged it? We know that redactors make such changes regularly.[3]

---

[2] To conclude to the presence of a source document on the basis of even a clear contradiction requires a logical leap: one must assume that a *redactor* overlooked a problem that an *author* would have noticed and avoided, though there is no compelling reason why a redactor should be more inept than an author in this regard. Nevertheless, while that conclusion is not inevitable, historical critics deem that the cumulative weight of the evidence favors it in many cases. On the other hand, a different objection—an *a priori* denial of any contradictions at all—is specious. True, it is always possible to explain away apparent contradictions (arguing, for example, that Gen 6:19 means only that Noah should collect the animals in breeding pairs, while 7:2 specifies how many breeding pairs of each species). But the very fact that such ingenious explanations are needed points up that, on its plainest reading, the text is at odds with itself.

[3] Fortunately, we have several examples in the biblical text of passages that are clearly dependent on a common source, and we can see how one or another transmitter has modified one or another of the versions. Compare, for instance, the two versions of the Ten Commandments (Exod 20:2-17 and Deut 5:6-21), or 2 Samuel 22:2-51 with Psalm 18:2-50, or 2 Samuel

Absent the original sources, how can redactional modifications be identified? Transitional passages help. These are passages, generally short, that attempt to join material from different sources either by reconciling tensions in the sources (see Gen 7:8-9!) or by connecting two unrelated passages narratively.[4] Such transitions are, in the main, redactors' creations, and sometimes they will reveal vocabulary, style, or concepts that are characteristic of the redactor. If these things then crop up again in the putative source material they can be scrutinized more closely as possible redactional modifications. Further, gaps in a reconstructed source document may indicate something missing that the redactor has omitted (e.g., source analysis of the Deluge account in Genesis 6–9 yields two older versions, but only one of them has an account of the actual building of the ark), or something that the redactor has reorganized.[5] Identifying the redactor's hand sets the starting point for redaction criticism, which we will discuss in greater detail in a moment.

Finally, source criticism strives to reconstruct, insofar as it is possible, the original source document. Redactional additions are removed; redactional omissions are tentatively filled—at least in general substance and perhaps, very tentatively, in wording; suspected rearrangements are put back to their presumed original order; wording characteristic of the redactor is noted as arguably unoriginal; and so forth. More importantly—and more constructively—source materials from different passages (e.g., from the creation accounts in Genesis 1–2 and the Deluge accounts in Genesis 6–9) are scrutinized for verbal and/or ideological links that might point to a source document that encompassed more than a single story.[6]

24:1-2 with 1 Chronicles 21:1-2 (where the Chronicler changes an original "YHWH" to "Satan"!), or Matthew 19:9 with Luke 16:18. Determining the wording of the original is not always possible. but when it can be done with some likelihood, then redactional modifications can be identified as well.

[4] 1 Kings 18:19-20, for instance, is often considered a redactional creation intended to link the story of Ahab and Elijah and the end of the drought (18:1-18, 41-46) with an originally independent story of a contest between Elijah and the prophets of Baal on top of Mount Carmel (18:21-40). For a presentation of this position see Simon J. DeVries, *1 Kings,* WBC 12 (Waco: Word Books, 1985) 206–10, 223–31. (I will argue below that 18:18b should also be considered redactional; see n. 8, p. 94.)

[5] For example, in one reconstructed source document of the Deluge story, Genesis 7:12 ("And rain fell upon the earth forty days and forty nights") is immediately adjacent to Genesis 7:16b ("And YHWH shut him in"). In the extant, combined text, the order of the two sentences makes perfect sense. But it is likely that, in the original document, the two sentences were in reverse order, since YHWH would have shut Noah and his family in the ark *before* the forty days and nights of rain began.

[6] For example, there are many verbal and conceptual connections between one Deluge source document and the creation story in Genesis 1. Once this is seen, it becomes clear that

Once the original source document has been reconstructed, it can be studied like any other ancient document. Naturally one can never ignore either the hypothetical nature of the reconstructed source or its incomplete state; these factors mean that any inferences one draws carry a heavy freight of tentativeness. But such a reconstructed document, hypothetical as it may be, is all we have; and as long as it is used with due caution it is better than nothing. And so the scholar searches it for clues to its dating, its worldview, what it can tell us about the society that produced it and about the people and events it depicts, and so on.

It is clear that source criticism is of profound importance for historical investigation. When we manage to recreate an ancient document, even tentatively, we open a line of sight on an otherwise lost past. This is the process, for example, that yielded some of the historical data we relied on in Part One, such as the length of Ahab's reign. That information comes from 1 Kings 16:29, but it is held by many scholars (though, indeed, not by all) to go back to contemporary or near-contemporary sources (e.g., perhaps to the "Book of the Annals of the Kings of Israel" mentioned in 1 Kings 22:39). When a reconstructed source document appears to be contemporary or near-contemporary to the people and events it portrays, the historian can use it to support historical reconstruction.

Redaction Criticism

Redaction criticism begins from the second step of source criticism, the identification of modifications the redactor made in preexisting source documents. It is less interested in the source documents themselves, and more interested in what the modifications can tell us about what was important to the redactor. Redaction criticism's basic question is "Why?"— why did the redactor add to, leave out from, reword, or rearrange the source?[7] Answers, of course, are necessarily conjectural; redactors have not left us commentaries on their work any more than other ancient authors

---

the two stories correspond to one another in profound theological ways, and that a single original source document (conventionally called the "Priestly Source") presented the Deluge as a systematic reversal of the creation account (the waters above and below are rejoined; the dry land is submerged in the waters; all categories of living creatures—except fish, naturally!—are drowned) followed by a new creation (the creative "wind" or "spirit" in 8:1b corresponds to that in 1:2b) with a new grant of food (9:3-4 corresponds to 1:30) and blessing of fruitfulness (9:1, 7 corresponds to 1:28a) and of dominion (9:2 corresponds to 1:28b).

[7] In theory the question can also be asked about material left unchanged: Why did the redactor find this material satisfactory as it stood? In practice, redaction criticism has paid much less attention to this question.

have. And proposed answers can cover a vast range of significance, from simple stylistic improvement to profound ideological commitments. The test of any single answer's cogency is the same one we have invoked repeatedly in the past: coherence. Does this answer contribute to making sense of the text as a whole? For example, is a propensity for "stylistic improvement" broadly characteristic of the work of this particular redactor? Or is the theological or political attitude proposed to explain a particular change attested elsewhere in other changes made by the same redactor?

Clearly, solid redaction-critical hypotheses can be erected only on solid source-critical foundations. Accurately distinguishing the redactor's modifications from the preexisting source documents is essential. Redaction criticism's results, then, are even more conjectural than source criticism's, since the substructure of the former's speculations is supplied by the already speculative results of the latter. However, here too we have no choice. If we wish to trace the history of a text's composition (and certainly that project is worth undertaking), there is no other way to go about it.

Redaction criticism has its own peculiar complexities as well. Our biblical texts have probably undergone several redactional stages—and these must be carefully separated from one another, since each redactor is likely to have a different agenda. Redaction criticism treats each presumed level of redaction as a unique document, assignable, theoretically, to a unique historical setting. Concerns revealed by redactional modifications can help date the redactional level; then what we know independently about Israelite history can supply a fuller context for interpreting the whole text at this stage of its development. Redaction criticism, therefore, does not directly aid in discovering anything about the historical accuracy of the people and events depicted in the source text; that is the thrust of source criticism. Redaction criticism reveals, rather, how stories, transmitted from generation to generation, change, both to mirror and to speak to the societies that transmit them.

King Ahab: The Oldest Information

In Part One we used the historical data source critics generally hold to be reliable. This information is found almost entirely in the opening and closing formulas for Ahab's reign (1 Kgs 16:29 and 22:39-40). The *formulation* is most likely due to the redactor, since very similar formulations occur with virtually every one of the thirty-some reigns recounted from 1 Kings 12 through to the end of 2 Kings. They appear to be the Deuteronomic Historian's way of organizing the story of the divided kingdoms. The *information,* however—such as the year of his accession, the length of the king's reign, the name of his capital city, and the name of his successor—is generally deemed to be much older,[8] perhaps going back to official court annals (if that is what the works to which the Historian refers were). The remark about Ahab's "ivory house" (22:39) is also likely to be much older; were it a redactional addition, reflective of an issue of particular concern to the redactor, we would expect it to figure somewhere in the rest of the Ahab story, but it does not. Archaeologists' unearthing of lavish ivory decorations from the Samaria of Ahab's time supports the antiquity of the remark.

Source and redaction criticism of the stories in 1 Kings 17:1–22:38, however, is much less straightforward. One recent scholar estimates that "[a] conservative tally . . . yields at least seventeen traditional oral and/or written sources and seven redactional hands and/or interpolators" in the passages dealing with Ahab.[9] Needless to say, an exhaustive study of material that complex is far beyond what we can attempt here. We will limit ourselves to just a few questions that will be both representative of historical critical study and illustrative of how that study can illumine the text's history.

---

[8] Not all of this information is equally reliable. Even within the Hebrew text, and especially between the standard Hebrew textual tradition and that reflected in the ancient Greek translation (the Septuagint), there are several discrepancies in accession years and lengths of reign. Whether these differences are due to intentional changes by redactors or to scribal errors in copying the manuscripts is unclear. Where the ancient sources do not agree, each item must be studied carefully. In the case of Ahab the only such problem in the opening and closing formulas is a difference in his year of accession. The standard Hebrew text says he came to the throne "in the thirty-eighth year of [the forty-one year reign of] Asa of Judah," while the Greek tradition dates his accession to "the second year of [Asa's son] Jehoshaphat." The problems connected with establishing the exact chronology of the kings of Israel and Judah are enormous, and the bibliography is daunting. For an overview of the issue see Mordechai Cogan, "Chronology," in David Noel Freedman et al., eds., *The Anchor Bible Dictionary* (New York: Doubleday, 1992) 1:1002–11.

[9] Brandon L. Fredenburg, *With Horns of Irony: The Implications of Irony in the Account of Ahab's Reign (1 Kings 16:29–22:40)*, Ph.D. dissertation, Iliff School of Theology and The University of Denver (Colorado Seminary), 2003 (Ann Arbor: University Microfilms, 2004) 49.

CHAPTER TWO

Ahab and the Prophets

One of the unexpected observations a careful reader of the books of Kings makes concerns the surprisingly frequent appearance of prophets, named and unnamed, in the account of the Divided Kingdoms. Historical critics speculate that stories about prophets, handed on within ancient Israelite prophetic groups that knew them, may have supplied the Deuteronomic Historian with a good deal of his traditional material.[1] The presence among these prophetic tales of many stories that have nothing to do with kings and their doings[2] supports this inference, since this is the sort of story unlikely to have been recorded in official annals.[3] Even when stories feature both prophets and kings (usually interacting with one another), prophetic circles are more likely to highlight the prophetic figure while official sources will tend to make the king more prominent.

---

[1] One scholar in particular, Antony F. Campbell, has argued in a series of works that this prophetic tradition took the form of a recoverable written document that he calls the "Prophetic Record." See *Of Prophets and Kings: A Late Ninth-Century Document (1 Samuel 1–2 Kings 10)*, CBQMS 17 (Washington, DC: Catholic Biblical Association of America, 1986), and Antony F. Campbell and Mark A. O'Brien, *Unfolding the Deuteronomic History: Origins, Upgrades, Present Text* (Minneapolis: Fortress, 2000) 24–33. See also Campbell's *1 Samuel*, FOTL 7 (Grand Rapids: Eerdmans, 2003).

[2] See, for instance, the stories of the prophet of Bethel and the man of God from Judah (1 Kgs 13:11-32), of Elijah and the widow (1 Kgs 17:8-24), of Elijah on Mount Horeb (1 Kgs 19:1-18), of Elijah and Elisha (1 Kgs 19:19-21; 2 Kgs 2:1-25), of Elisha and the prophetic guilds (2 Kgs 4:1-44), and many others.

[3] This is true whether the stories have historical basis or not. Stories of a popular prophet's great deeds among ordinary people are more likely to circulate among a prophet's disciples and admirers than among an often hostile political establishment, regardless of whether those stories are historical memories or pious fabrications.

As far as Ahab is concerned, he almost never appears without a prophet somewhere nearby. Only in 1 Kings 21:1-16 do we find a more or less self-contained narrative of Ahab with no prophetic presence; and, in the present form of the text, even that narrative leads directly into Elijah's condemnatory confrontation with Ahab in vv. 17-29. Most of Ahab's dealings with prophets, particularly with Elijah, are hostile. These include the story of the drought, which supplies the continuity for 1 Kings 17–19, and the story of Naboth in 1 Kings 21. Only in the first stories of the Aramean wars (1 Kings 20) do we find prophets sympathetic to Ahab (20:13-28), but these encounters are balanced by a negative one (20:35-43); and in the later story (1 Kings 22) the prophet Micaiah ben Imlah is entirely hostile to Ahab.[4]

Elijah and Ahab: The Story of the Drought

Chapters 17–19 of 1 Kings incorporate two types of material. The framework is supplied by the story of a drought that Elijah announces (17:1) and, eventually and on YHWH's command, brings to an end (18:1-18a, 41-46). King Ahab figures in every part of this story. Into it, however, have been intercalated several other stories of Elijah that have nothing to do either with Ahab or with the drought, or, often, with each other. These stories concern Elijah's private life (17:2-6, 8-24; 19:19-21), his contest with prophets of Baal on Mount Carmel (18:21-40), and his experience of a theophany on Mount Horeb (19:4-18).[5] There are a few redactional passages that smooth the transitions between the drought story and the other material (17:7;[6] 18:18b-20; 19:1-3).

---

[4] I do not number the "four hundred prophets" headed by Zedekiah ben Kenaanah in 1 Kings 22 among the sympathetic prophets because the story clearly presents them as toadies of the king. They do not represent, as Elijah does, the independent voice of prophecy (despite the fact that they are duped by YHWH's "lying spirit" into prophesying what YHWH wants them to speak!).

[5] Internal tensions indicate a complex prehistory for both types of material. For example, in the drought story the solitary Elijah of 18:7-16 suddenly acquires a servant in 18:41-44, and in the other material the starving widow of 17:12 is the owner of a two-story house in 17:17. It is most likely that the drought story took complete form already within prophetic circles. How and when the other materials came together and when they were joined to the drought story are harder to determine. Were they too combined with each other and with the drought story already by prophetic tradents, or did the Deuteronomic Historian receive them as separate blocks of tradition and combine them himself? Our only clues would come from the transitional passages, and they do not contain any elements that are decisively characteristic of either.

[6] 1 Kings 17:14b may also be redactional, though this is not so clear. Note that the phrase "until the day that the LORD sends rain on the earth" is not repeated when the rest of

There are no strong thematic links between the two bodies of material.[7] Particularly striking is the absence of any explicit anti-Baal polemic in the story of the drought,[8] and the complete absence of Ahab from the other material. In other words, though the earlier prophetic traditions that underlie 1 Kings 17–19 are certainly not sympathetic to Ahab, the characteristic of Ahab that stands out most prominently in the narrative as a whole, namely his active support of the worship of Baal, does *not* seem to have been noticeably present in its sources.

How, then, does that impression arise? The intercalation of the other material—most especially the contest between Elijah and the prophets of Baal, with its spectacular miracle and its blood-drenched climax—casts an aura over the entire passage and transforms "drought," an otherwise neutral component of the drought story, into a vehicle of the anti-Baal polemic. In a climate like Israel's, with virtually no agriculturally useful ground water, life depends—literally—on a sufficiency of rain. Drought means famine and ultimately starvation. This is the drama of the drought story taken alone. However, combined with a story about rivalry between YHWH and Baal, drought takes on deep theological significance. Baal was the Canaanite god of rain and storms, and his supremacy in that regard had been acknowledged for centuries in the lands at the eastern end of the Mediterranean. To announce YHWH's authority over those elements, as Elijah does in 17:1, and to demonstrate it, as he does in 18:41-46, is implicitly to attack Baal on his own turf and to challenge the central tenet of Baalist thought. Combining that announcement and demonstration with Elijah's challenge to the prophets of Baal (18:21-40) makes that attack explicit.

---

the divine promise is repeated in v. 16. If v. 14b is not redactional, it marks the only appearance of the "drought" motif in the non-Ahab material.

[7] Narrative criticism would nevertheless point to some subtler links—for instance, Ahab's exaction of an oath from neighboring kings (18:10) is ironic in view of the fact that Elijah was in Sidon, the kingdom of Ahab's father-in-law (17:8; 16:31) and the people's ready access to twelve jars of water (18:33-35) contrasts with Ahab's inability to locate any (18:5).

[8] 1 Kings 18:18b is only an apparent exception. The verse is marked by several irregularities that reveal a redactor's work. The second-person form in the phrase "you have forsaken the commandments" is in the plural, whereas that in "[you have] followed the Baals" is in the singular. The plural "Baals," which never occurs anywhere else in the books of Kings, also suggests that these words may be from an isolated hand. It is quite likely, then, that at least the last phrase of the verse ("and followed the Baals") is a very late redactional expansion. The redactor who inserted 18:19-20, with its reference to the "prophets of Baal," had already established a transition from the Ahab-drought story to the contest on Carmel; presumably a still later hand (betrayed by his idiosyncratic plural "Baals") tried to strengthen it by making explicit Ahab's connection with Baalism.

It is difficult, if not impossible, to determine whether this combination of anti-Baal polemic and drought story was first made by the Deuteronomic Historian—therefore several centuries after Ahab's death and of very dubious historical reliability—or at some earlier time by the prophetic circles within which both types of material were passed on. But what is apparent is that, as far as 1 Kings 17–19 is concerned, the picture of Ahab as a staunch proponent of Baalism over against Yahwism is a product of redactional activity, and does not form part of the original traditions. Can this picture be assigned reasonably to any particular stage in the development of Israelite religion?

To pursue this question we must pause briefly to summarize the present state of affairs in the study of the religious history of Israel. The student who is not aware of recent discussions in this area may be dismayed to learn that historians' reconstruction of that history differs significantly from the biblical picture. What follows will be necessarily oversimplified and presented without evidence or argumentation. The interested student is urged to consult other studies for a fuller discussion of the issues.[9]

EXCURSUS ON ISRAELITE RELIGION

Israelite culture, including Israelite religion, developed out of Canaanite culture and religion. The earliest discernible stages of Israelite religion in the premonarchic period reflect a recognition of the existence of many deities and a variety of strategies of assimilation[10] and differentiation to rationalize the relationships among them. During the monarchic period (late eleventh to early sixth centuries B.C.E.) YHWH gradually emerged as the dominant deity of the Israelites, supreme over all others and worshiped above them, though not at first to their exclusion. They were acknowledged as lesser deities subordinate to him. By the ninth century B.C.E., particularly among prophetic circles dedicated to the service of YHWH, voices were being raised to demand *exclusive* worship of YHWH. This demand did not rest on a belief in "monotheism" (that is, that only one God *exists*); the reality of other gods was not doubted. But it did seek to exclude the worship

[9] A particularly useful source in this respect is Mark S. Smith, *The Early History of God: YHWH and the Other Deities in Ancient Israel,* 2nd ed. (Grand Rapids: Eerdmans, 2002).

[10] For example, the originally distinct gods YHWH and El came to be identified with one another.

of all deities except YHWH as "foreign," including even the indigenous Canaanite deities Baal and Asherah. The demand for exclusive worship—technically called "monolatry"—is attested in the prophetic traditions associated with Elijah and Elisha and in the prophecies of Hosea a century later. By the late seventh century B.C.E., with the adoption of the principles of Deuteronomy in the reform under King Josiah of Judah, what had begun as the comparatively extreme view of an intolerant minority prevailed and was established as orthodoxy. Exclusive worship of YHWH was now considered the norm, and deviation from that norm was officially condemned. This is the ideology that underlies the Deuteronomic History and according to which the Deuteronomic Historian rendered his theological judgments on all the past monarchs of Israel and Judah. Finally, during—and in theological response to—the Babylonian Exile (587–537 B.C.E.), thinkers such as "Second Isaiah" (the author of Isaiah 40–55) came to articulate the belief that no gods other than YHWH truly exist—"monotheism" in its classic formulation.

This reconstruction of Israelite religious history supplies a context within which the development we have proposed for 1 Kings 17–19 fits comfortably, though it does not supply answers for all our questions. Ahab, in the ninth century B.C.E., would have offered royal support to the various deities worshiped in Israel—a perfectly acceptable practice at the time.[11] However, among the prophets of Ahab's day or perhaps of his sons', there was a movement in favor of exclusive worship of YHWH. This accounts for the anti-Baal polemic of the story of Elijah and the prophets of Baal on Mount Carmel. From the point of view of such exclusivist prophets, Ahab's support of the cult of Baal would have been intolerable. That would easily have led to traditions in which Ahab figured negatively, like the drought story. It may also have led to combining the Carmel story with the drought story, by which the prophets' disdain for Ahab would be explicitly linked to his support of Baal. On the other hand, centuries later, when the orthodoxy of exclusive worship of YHWH had prevailed, the Deuteronomic Historian would have had equal reason to take that step if it had not already been done.

[11] Whether his personal devotion was directed primarily to YHWH or to Baal is not remembered, though it is perhaps telling that both of his known sons (Ahaziah and Jehoram) bear names that acknowledge YHWH. If Athaliah is his daughter (2 Kgs 8:18) rather than the daughter of Omri (2 Kgs 8:26, despite the *NRSV*'s interpretive translation "granddaughter"; see n. 1 to Part One), then all three of Ahab's known children bear Yahwistic names.

Redaction criticism of 1 Kings 17–19, then, suggests that the early prophetic movement, perhaps even contemporary with Ahab, was hostile to him. However, it leaves open the question of whether that hostility was rooted in Ahab's (historically probable) support of the cult of Baal or in some other perceived malfeasance. The former is quite plausible, given what we believe we know about the history of Israelite religion, but uncertainty about the composition history of the text allows for other possibilities as well.

Elijah and Ahab: The Story of Naboth

The situation in 1 Kings 21 is different. Here the negative story about Ahab (21:1-16) shows no evidence of prophetic origins, nor does it contain any indications of royal patronage for the Baalist enterprise. On the contrary, the religious aspects of the text (for example, the legal prescriptions and ritual practices Jezebel invokes) are thoroughly Yahwist, and Ahab's acknowledgment of the law of ancestral inheritance (however grudging that acknowledgment may have been) bespeaks an awareness of and compliance with Yahwistic law.

There is very little in 21:1-16 to identify the origin, date, or transmission history of the story. One potential indicator is the particular hostility the story shows toward Jezebel, centering blame on her rather than on Ahab. If it were possible to establish a context for a redactor with this fixation, that could suggest a dating for the whole story, since Jezebel's central role is integral to the narrative. The clearest instance of anti-Jezebel rhetoric elsewhere in the Ahab story is 16:31, which is almost certainly to be attributed to the Deuteronomic Historian in the late seventh century. On the other hand, the claim that Jezebel murdered prophets of YHWH and supported prophets of Baal is apparently[12] found already in the material transmitted by the prophetic circles (see 18:4, 13), and there is evidence elsewhere in the books of Kings of early prophetic condemnation of her (1 Kgs 21:23; 2 Kgs 9:36-37). And so the evidence does not permit any solid inferences about the origins of this specific narrative.

[12] It is not entirely certain that these remarks about Jezebel, which are contained in a parenthetical description of Obadiah (18:3b-4) and an extensive speech attributed to him (18:9-14), are original parts of the prophetic material. The elaboration of such a minor character as Obadiah (he never appears anywhere else in the Hebrew Bible) may be a theological maneuver by the redactor who joined the drought story to the contest story. See my *1 Kings*, Berit Olam: Studies in Biblical Hebrew Narrative and Poetry (Collegeville: Liturgical Press, 1996) 237–42, 258–60. Similarly, the mention of Jezebel in 18:19 comes from the redactor who joined those two stories.

A second potential indication of date is the crime itself. Jehu's words in 2 Kings 9:25-26 testify that *some* version of a royal crime against Naboth was part of a very early tradition received by the Deuteronomic Historian.[13] But what is attested there has important differences from what we see in 1 Kings 21. In 2 Kings 9:25-26 Jezebel is not remembered as a perpetrator, Elijah is not remembered as the bearer of the word of condemnation, and Naboth's sons are killed along with their father.[14] All of this suggests that the version of the Naboth story we have in 1 Kings 21:1-16 is a later elaboration of an earlier tradition, and that the introduction of Jezebel and Elijah (and Ahab? see n. 14) into the story reflects the redactor's antipathy for the house of Ahab rather than received historical information.

The remainder of the chapter is quite complex. Detailed treatments of all the elements in 1 Kings 21:17-29 would require a major monograph.[15] The similarities and explicit cross references that link 21:21-22, 24 (and 2 Kgs 9:7-9) with oracles against Jeroboam (1 Kgs 14:10-11) and Baasha (16:3-4) make it indubitable that the Deuteronomic Historian has intervened in the wording, but that does not rule out a tradition, *independent of the Naboth story,* of a prophetic oracle to some or all of these three kings announcing the end of their dynasties. The oracle against Jezebel (21:23) is echoed in 2 Kings 9:10 and 9:36, but there is nothing explicit in the oracle that identifies her wrongdoing either as the crime against Naboth or as Baalism. The prediction of Ahab's death (21:19b) is partially but inaccurately fulfilled in 22:38 and more fully, but still inaccurately, in 2 Kings 9:25-26.[16] And the deferral of Ahab's punishment to the days of his son (21:27-29) is at odds with his violent death in 22:35-37, though it agrees

---

[13] The story of Jehu (2 Kings 9–10) is usually thought to have been composed to justify and support Jehu's seizure of power. This would argue in favor of a date fairly soon after the coup d'état, which probably occurred during the 840s B.C.E., less than fifteen years after Ahab's death.

[14] The wording of 9:25 is quite awkward in Hebrew. This has led at least one scholar to conclude that the phrase "when you and I rode side by side behind his father Ahab" is a later, redactional insertion. If that is the case, then not even *Ahab* is mentioned in the original form of this tradition. See J. M. Miller, "The Fall of the House of Ahab," *Vetus Testamentum* 17 (1967) 307–24. Miller proposes that the Naboth event *is* historical, but that it occurred many years after Ahab's death, during the reign of his son Jehoram.

[15] See, for example, Reinhold Bohlen's *Der Fall Nabot: Form, Hintergrund und Werdegang einer alttestamentlichen Erzählung (1 Kön 21),* Trierer Theologische Studien 35 (Trier: Paulinus-Verlag, 1978), which runs to over 450 pages.

[16] In 1 Kings 22:38 the dogs lick up Ahab's blood, as YHWH had decreed in 21:19b, but they do not do so *in Jezreel,* "the place where dogs licked up the blood of Naboth" (21:19b), but "by the pool of Samaria" (22:38). And there is no mention in 21:19b of "prostitutes washing themselves" in the blood of Ahab, as 22:38 claims the oracle foretold. In 2 Kings 9:25-26 King Jehoram (not Ahab!) is thrown onto "the plot of ground belonging to Naboth

with Jehu's claim that the death of Jehoram fulfilled the prophetic oracle against Ahab (2 Kgs 9:25-26). (We will look at this discrepancy more closely in the next chapter.)

What can we conclude from this dizzying array of comparisons and conjectures? First, there is clear evidence of early hostility to the rule of the house of Ahab, and not just on the part of prophets. Jehu's bloody coup d'état in the 840s, which wiped out the entire house of Ahab, enjoyed military support and the support of a group called the Rechabites as well.[17] But it is unclear whether that opposition reaches back to the days of Ahab himself or developed only later, during the brief reign of Ahab's son, Ahaziah (2 Kings 1), or the longer reign of Ahab's second son, Jehoram. In either case it is not far removed from Ahab's own days. Second, some crime against an Israelite landholder was laid to the account of royal injustice. But, again, the possibility that Ahab's part in that crime is the product of later, hostile redaction cannot be ruled out. Jehoram, with or without the collusion of Jezebel, his queen mother, may have been the guilty party. And third, Jezebel, Ahab's foreign wife, was a target of particular vituperation in some circles, particularly among the prophets; their antipathy, however, is most easily explained by their insistence on exclusive worship of YHWH confronted with Jezebel's understandable support for the Baalist cult of her homeland. There is nothing in our earliest retrievable traditions to affirm or deny her role in the judicial murder of Naboth, and the possibility that (prophetic?) circles hostile to her associated her with that crime in order to further blacken her name is entirely plausible.

Ahab and Other Prophets: The Aramean Wars

The remaining stories of Ahab (1 Kings 20; 22) involve several prophetic figures, though Elijah is not one of them. In the next chapter we shall look at these stories from a different angle, concentrating on them as records of political history. Here we want to focus on what we can determine about their origins and transmission in prophetic circles and the extent to which the ideology of those circles may have redactionally transformed them in the process of transmission.

---

the Jezreelite," presumably to lie unburied for consumption by scavengers, in line with what was foretold in 21:24.

[17] Little is said about the Rechabites in the Hebrew Bible, but they seem to have been fanatical opponents of the worship of Baal (see 2 Kgs 10:15-17, 23-25), and traditionalists in their style of life (see Jeremiah 35).

As we discussed above, source and redaction criticism begin by observing points of tension within the smoothness and coherence of the text. That tension may involve discrepancies in vocabulary, in literary style, in ideological outlook, in factual information, etc. One area redaction criticism has not often attended to is literary structure; this is, at least in part, because realization of the importance of structure—particularly symmetrical structure—in biblical Hebrew narrative is relatively recent.[18] Discernment of symmetry in 1 Kings 20 and 22, however, leads to important redaction critical insights.

In Part Two we saw that both chapters dealing with the Aramean wars combine material highly favorable to Ahab with prophetic passages that condemn him roundly. In each chapter the favorable material forms a complete, self-contained story with symmetrical structure; the negative material constitutes either an addendum (in chapter 20) or an interruption (in chapter 22) to that structure. If symmetrical structuring of narrative is as pervasive in biblical Hebrew prose as many scholars are now proposing,[19] then the departure from symmetry that marks these negative passages, supported by the contrast between positive and negative attitudes toward Ahab, can plausibly serve as evidence for the composite character of these chapters. In that case, what inferences can be drawn about the sources of their stories and their composition history?

In Part Two we mentioned in passing the symmetrical structure of 1 Kings 20:1-34. It has four parts, arranged in a chiasm (ABB'A'). The "A" sections involve negotiations between Ben-hadad and Ahab; the "B" sections recount the battles of Samaria and Aphek respectively. The story reaches satisfying closure with v. 34. All of this points to a self-contained narrative, independent of vv. 35-43. Since the addendum presupposes the narrative, but not vice versa, we may surmise that the story in 20:1-34 is older, and that the episodes in vv. 35-43 are a later redactional expansion.

The situation is similar in 1 Kings 22. Without the negative material in vv. 5-28 the story is complete, self-contained, and symmetrical. The structure is concentric:

---

[18] For further discussion see my *Style and Structure in Biblical Hebrew Narrative* (Collegeville: Liturgical Press, 2001).

[19] There are a large number of recent books and articles investigating and, largely, supporting this contention. Among them, David A. Dorsey, *The Literary Structure of the Old Testament: A Commentary on Genesis–Malachi* (Grand Rapids: Baker Book House, 1999) is perhaps the most ambitious. It seeks to identify symmetries in every book of the Hebrew Bible. For the Deuteronomic History see the detailed studies in the four volumes by Jan P. Fokkelman, *Narrative Art and Poetry in the Books of Samuel: A Full Interpretation Based on Stylistic and Structural Analyses* (Assen: Van Gorcum, 1981–1993).

A. In Samaria, Ahab prepares for war (22:1-4)
  B. Ahab's strategy is disguise (22:29-31)
    C. The battle (22:32-34)
  B'. Ahab's death is disguised (22:35)
A'. In Samaria, the king is buried (22:36-38a).[20]

Here, too, the anti-Ahab insertion (vv. 5-28) presupposes the surrounding narrative, but not vice versa. So we may infer that the pro-Ahab story is older, and that the expansion is redactional.

What is the origin of the pro-Ahab stories? Note, first, that there is no prophetic presence at all in 22:1-4, 29-38a. It is unlikely, therefore, that this story forms part of the traditions of prophetic circles that the Deuteronomic Historian received. And while two[21] prophets of YHWH figure in the pro-Ahab story of 1 Kings 20:1-34, they do so quite differently from prophets in the other Ahab narratives. Compare the presentation of the prophets here with Elijah in chapters 17–19, with the negative prophet in 20:35-43, and with Micaiah ben Imlah in 22:5-28. In all those cases the prophets have a dimension of individuality apart from being royal advisors. Elijah and Micaiah have names; Elijah features in a whole series of exploits not connected with the court; the prophet of 20:35-43 is a member of a prophetic guild and interacts with others in that guild (20:35-37); we see Micaiah in conversation with a royal messenger (22:13-14) and in conflict with other prophets (22:24-25).[22] Such a focus on the prophet as an individual warrants the inference that these stories have roots in prophetic

[20] There are likely redactional interventions in the last few verses. The remark about washing the chariot (v. 38a) seems intended to introduce the rest of v. 38, which is negative toward Ahab. And if v. 38 is redactional, then v. 35b certainly is too. It is also possible that v. 36 may be redactional. Although it is not explicitly anti-Ahab, it could be an anti-Ahab redactor's attempt to link Ahab's death with the prophecy of Micaiah in v. 17. At a minimum, then, the original account of Ahab's death and burial would have comprised vv. 35a and 37. Finally, the Hebrew text's use of an active form ("the king *came* to Samaria," v. 37a) instead of the passive supplied by the *NRSV* ("the king *was brought* to Samaria") may be a redactional modification; see above, p. 75.

[21] The first prophet appears in 20:13; he is introduced rather indefinitely as "a certain prophet." The prophet who appears in 20:22 is, presumably, the same person, since he is introduced as "the" prophet, not as "a" or "another" prophet. Finally, a "man of God" (a term used in Hebrew as a synonym for "prophet") addresses Ahab in 20:28. In this case, the individual may or may not be the same as the earlier "prophet" (the Hebrew could be translated "a man of God" or "the man of God"). We will assume that the change of terminology from "prophet" to "man of God" indicates a different person. This is not certain, but it is not pivotal for our analysis.

[22] There is also a reminder in v. 28b that Micaiah spoke other words as well. From a historical-critical point of view, however, this odd remark is not likely to be an original part of the text. Scholars point out that it is a quotation of the opening words of the book of the

circles, where the prophets themselves would have been of immediate interest. By contrast the prophets in 20:1-34 show no such development as individuals. They speak divine words to the king and there is nothing else to be said about them. They are little more than functions, comparable to the "messengers" of Ben-hadad in 20:2 and 5. There is nothing about these prophets that would point to prophetic circles as the original home of traditions about them.

By contrast the negative stories feature prophets as central figures, and they display the same sort of unique individuality we saw in Elijah as well as the same antipathy toward Ahab. It seems entirely reasonable to attribute them to prophetic circles like those that we surmise lie behind the Elijah stories. It is noteworthy that there is no mention of Baalism in either of the negative passages. In 20:35-43 the prophet condemns Ahab for not sealing his victory over Aram by killing King Ben-hadad. In 22:5-28 Micaiah announces YHWH's intention to destroy Ahab, but gives no reason for it. In this regard the stories' attitude toward Ahab is closest to that in the drought story of 1 Kings 17–18.

We deduced that the pro-Ahab stories are earlier than the negative episodes a redactor has used to transform them into condemnations of Ahab. This means that, on the basis of the evidence we have examined so far, there appear to have existed positive traditions about Ahab at least as old, if not older, than the negative ones transmitted in prophetic circles. Since these positive stories have their origin outside those prophetic circles we will defer closer study of them until the next chapter. There we will see that, despite their likely early date, they may in fact have nothing to tell us about Ahab at all.

In discussing the Naboth story we saw that negative prophetic attitudes toward the *house* of Ahab, if not to King Ahab himself, are likely to go back to shortly after Jehu's seizure of power, less than fifteen years after Ahab's death. It is possible that negative attitudes toward Ahab himself may go back that far, in which case they would be "contemporary or near-contemporary" to Ahab's reign. On the other hand, it is equally possible that they are later developments, transferring the prophetic hostility toward the sons to the father, and that only the negative attitudes toward the ruling house are "contemporary or near-contemporary" to the times they depict. Nothing in these stories enables us to resolve this question.

---

prophet Micah. They then explain it as a gloss—perhaps originally a marginal comment that a later copyist incorporated into the text—intended by a redactor or glossator to imply that Micaiah ("mikah-Yah") is identical to the similarly named Micah ("mikah") of Moresheth.

Conclusion

Source- and redaction-critical study of the Ahab stories reveals that these stories form only part of a larger set of traditions, not always in agreement with one another, that touch directly or indirectly upon King Ahab. Some of the incompatibilities are seen only when one compares the Ahab stories in 1 Kings with fragmentary traditions from 2 Kings such as the recollection of the Naboth story in 2 Kings 9:25-26. Others remain as points of tension within the Ahab stories themselves (e.g., 1 Kgs 21:29 versus 22:34-37; 1 Kgs 21:19b versus 22:38). A few of the stories are positive toward Ahab; the majority are severely negative. We have not yet determined the origin of the positive traditions; this will occupy us in the next chapter. Many, though not all (e.g., 21:1-16), of the negative stories seem to have their origin in prophetic circles, as do the fragmentary traditions in 2 Kings as well.

Relating the negative prophetic attitudes toward Ahab himself (1 Kings) to those that have the reigning house of Ahab in view (2 Kings) is difficult. Jehu's coup d'état in the 840s is a likely context for hostility to the house of Ahab; stories and traditions expressing that hostility would have circulated as a form of justification for Jehu's seizure of power and the bloodbath that ensued. Negative prophetic attitudes specifically directed at Ahab could be independent—or even the wellspring—of those against Ahab's house, but they could also be transferred secondarily to Ahab as ancestor of the hated house. According to at least one critic this is what happened in the non-prophetic story of 1 Kings 21:1-16 (see n. 14 above).

Motivations for the negative prophetic attitude are not always clear. In the drought story of 1 Kings 17:1; 18:1-18a, 41-46, Elijah does not explain what Ahab has done to deserve the drought. In 18:18a he accuses Ahab of "troubling Israel," but only the redactional expansion in v. 18b specifies what that troubling entailed. In 1 Kings 20:35-43 Ahab's wrong is not killing Ben-hadad; in 1 Kings 22:5-28 it is unspecified. Most notable is that the explicit anti-Baalist polemic of the prophetic traditions (e.g., 18:21-40; 19:18) existed independent of the Ahab stories and has been attached to them only redactionally (e.g., 18:18-20). This redactional development too may tentatively be assigned to the reign of Jehu, who is remembered in 2 Kings as champion of the fanatically Yahwist Rechabites and enemy of all things Baalist.

CHAPTER THREE

The Aramean Wars

A combination of factors—all of which we mentioned in the last chapter—makes the stories of Ahab and the Aramean wars (1 Kgs 20:1-34; 22:1-4, 29-38a) stand out from the rest of the material about Ahab. First, these stories are positive toward Ahab; the others are, without exception, negative. Second, there are no significant prophetic characters present in these stories; with the exception of 21:1-16, prophets figure in all the other passages that involve Ahab. This suggests an origin for these stories outside the prophetic circles that lie behind most of the other Ahab traditions. Third, there is no indication that these stories are late, and the presence of plausibly early redactional changes argues that they may be very early indeed, perhaps even "contemporary or near-contemporary" to Ahab himself. All together, these factors warrant a closer look at the two passages.

The first thing a closer look reveals is that these passages pose two fundamental historical problems. The first problem concerns the political relationship between Aram and Israel during the last years of Ahab's reign. The biblical picture is in serious tension with non-biblical historical evidence. The second problem concerns Ahab's death. Here the biblical text is in tension with itself, though the terms of the disagreement are not immediately apparent to the reader. We must examine both problems carefully if we are to do justice to what these stories can tell us about Ahab.

Israel and Aram

The biblical account of relations between Aram and Israel in the last years of Ahab's reign is straightforward. Four years before Ahab's death he was in vassalage to Ben-hadad, king of Aram. When Ben-hadad mounted an unprovoked and potentially devastating attack on Israel, Ahab responded militarily and inflicted a great defeat on Aram at Samaria (1 Kgs 20:1-21). A year later Ben-hadad attacked Ahab again at Aphek. This time Aram's military might was crushed. Even allowing for Israelite boasting and exaggeration, claiming 127,000 Aramean casualties (1 Kgs 20:29-30) is tantamount to claiming that Ben-hadad's forces were wiped out completely.[1] In the aftermath of that defeat Ben-hadad was reduced to suing for vassal status to Ahab, but Ahab magnanimously treated him as an equal instead. The two kings concluded a treaty that was quite favorable to Ahab, the victor, without being oppressive to Ben-hadad. Three years later, claiming that Ben-hadad had not kept his part of the treaty, Ahab attacked him at Ramoth Gilead (1 Kgs 22:29). In this battle—whose outcome is not clear in the text—Ahab was killed by mishap (1 Kgs 22:34-37).

Though the biblical picture is clear, it is almost impossible to reconcile with our independent historical evidence. The battle of Qarqar took place in 853 B.C.E.; Assyrian forces under Shalmaneser III attacked a coalition of West Asian states headed by Hadad-ezer, the king of Aram. Shalmaneser boasts of his victory in the Monolith Inscription[2] and names Ahab as part of the coalition ranged against him. If our biblical information about dates of royal accession and length of reigns is at all reliable, Ahab must have died in that same year.[3] This means that in the very year that he was a subordinate coalition member cooperating with King Hadad-ezer of Aram at Qarqar, he was also an aggressor attacking King Ben-hadad of Aram at Ramoth Gilead! Even if we allow that "Hadad-ezer" and "Ben-hadad" might be the same person (a conjecture for which there is no supportive evidence), it is difficult to reconcile Ahab's role in the coalition with an attack on Aramean holdings as described in 1 Kings 22. It is also difficult to reconcile Aram's leadership of the coalition at Qarqar with the near destruction of its military forces three years previously at Aphek, as depicted in 1 Kings 20. Is it possible to resolve this conflicting information? Before we attempt to answer that question, we must examine our second historical problem: How did Ahab die?

---

[1] For comparative purposes, at the battle of Qarqar in 853 B.C.E. the Arameans, who were the most powerful force in the coalition that opposed Shalmaneser III, were able to field 20,000 troops; Israel fielded 10,000.

[2] On the Monolith Inscription and the battle of Qarqar see above, p. 5. Historians suspect strongly that Shalmaneser's boast is pure bravado, and that the battle was at best a stalemate for the Assyrians, if not a defeat.

[3] It is unlikely that Ahab died at the battle of Qarqar. Had Shalmaneser killed one of the opposing kings, he surely would have made mention of it in his inscriptions.

The Dilemma of Ahab's Death

Again the biblical evidence seems straightforward. Ahab was killed in the battle of Ramoth Gilead. A careful reading of two other passages, however, reveals a contrary tradition that Ahab died peacefully. First, in 1 Kings 22:40 the Deuteronomic Historian tells us that "Ahab slept with his ancestors." This statement is part of the Historian's framework for the history of the Divided Kingdoms; in all likelihood it comes originally from the archival sources to which the Historian seems to have had access.[4] That euphemistic formula for a king's death, however, is never used for a king who died by violence.[5] Second, the word of YHWH to Ahab in 1 Kings 21:29 points to a peaceful death for Ahab rather than the violent death predicted in 21:19. And that tradition is supported by Jehu's remark in 2 Kings 9:25-26, which identifies Jehoram's death as the fulfillment of the oracular punishment for the crime against Naboth.

Obviously Ahab could not have died both peacefully and by violence. Since the Deuteronomic Historian's notice that he "slept with his ancestors" probably comes from archival material (i.e., near-contemporary to Ahab), it enjoys much more claim to historical reliability. How, then, could the tradition of Ahab's death in battle—and the whole story of which it is the dramatic climax—have arisen? The problem has long exercised historians, and several scholars have come to question whether these stories were originally about Ahab at all.

Ahab?

Notice something odd: In 1 Kings 22:1-38, King Jehoshaphat of Judah is named by name every time he appears (a total of thirteen times). By contrast, the king of Aram is *never* named, and the king of Israel is named only once (22:20)—even in coordinated phrases like "The king of Israel and King Jehoshaphat of Judah" (22:10, 29)! The suspicion arises that either the names of the Israelite and Aramean kings have been suppressed from the tradition or the name of Jehoshaphat has been added. Somewhat similarly, in 1 Kings 20, although the Aramean king, Benhadad, is named regularly, Ahab is named only in vv. 2, 13, and 14; otherwise he is "the king of Israel" (eight times in vv. 1-34).[6]

---

[4] See the remarks above, p. 90, under "King Ahab: The Oldest Information."

[5] On 2 Kings 14:22 as an apparent exception to this pattern see n. 72 on p. 76.

[6] This does not count the appearance (in the *NRSV*) in v. 34, since that is not found in the Hebrew. See the remarks above, p. 43. In the redactional expansion (vv. 35-43) he is "king of Israel" three times, and simply "the king" three times, but never "Ahab."

Putting all the evidence together about Aram-Israel relations, Ahab's death, and the relative anonymity of the Israelite king in these chapters, the German scholar Alfred Jepsen first proposed that the stories in 1 Kings 20 may have originally had in view some later Israelite king and only subsequently been transferred to Ahab in the process of transmission.[7] Since that time many other scholars have taken up the suggestion, with some modifications, and extended it to include the story in 1 Kings 22 as well.[8] There is some disagreement as to which king was original to the stories, Jehoahaz (813–797 B.C.E.) or his son Joash (796–781 B.C.E.),[9] but those who support this hypothesis agree that it was a king of the dynasty founded by Jehu, not a descendant of Ahab.[10] Reasons include the fact that relations between Aram and Israel during the Jehu dynasty were hostile (see 2 Kgs 10:32-33; 13:1-25), with Israel less powerful than Aram (2 Kgs 13:7); that the king of Aram during Ahab's day was Hadad-ezer, according to Shalmaneser's Monolith Inscription, but the king of Aram in the days of Joash (and perhaps during Jehoahaz's days as well) was named Ben-hadad (2 Kgs 13:3, 24-25); and that there are points of convergence between the stories of 1 Kings 20 and those of the later period that suggest a single origin for the variant traditions.[11]

---

[7] Jepsen proposed this in "Israel und Damaskus," *Archiv für Orientforschung* 14 (1942) 153–72.

[8] In particular J. Maxwell Miller has worked out the proposal in a series of studies: "The Elisha Cycle and the Accounts of the Omride Wars," *Journal of Biblical Literature* 85 (1966) 441–55; "The Fall of the House of Ahab," *Vetus Testamentum* 17 (1967) 307–24; "The Rest of the Acts of Jehoahaz (I KINGS 20; 22:1-38)," *Zeitschrift für die alttestamentliche Wissenschaft* 80 (1968) 337–42. See also the discussions in John Gray, *I & II Kings,* 2nd ed. (Philadelphia: Westminster, 1970) 414–18, and J. Alberto Soggin, *An Introduction to the History of Israel and Judah,* 2nd ed. (Valley Forge, PA: Trinity Press International, 1993) 218–19.

[9] The theory is not without difficulties, of course. One is that both Jehoahaz and Joash "slept with their fathers"—that is, they died peacefully—according to the Deuteronomic Historian (2 Kgs 13:9, 13). The difficulty is not insurmountable, but it would take us too far afield to address it here.

[10] Thus the stories would have originated a half century or more after Ahab's death in 853 B.C.E. The redactional transfer of the story from its original royal figure to Ahab would be even later. If the original form of the story could be reconstructed it might serve as a contemporary or near-contemporary source of evidence for Jehoahaz or Joash, but not for Ahab.

[11] For example, compare 1 Kings 20:34 ("I will restore the towns that my father took from your father") with 2 Kings 13:25 ("Jehoash son of Jehoahaz took again from Ben-hadad son of Hazael the towns that he had taken from his father Jehoahaz in war"). Note also that Aphek is a scene of battle in both passages (1 Kgs 20:26; 2 Kgs 13:17). There is a further detail that, at first glance, appears to cinch the case, though in fact it does not. Ahab turns Micaiah ben Imlah over to the custody of "Joash, the king's son" (1 Kgs 22:26). We know of no son of Ahab by that name, but Jehoahaz had a son Joash, who succeeded him on

Operating on this hypothesis—that the stories of war between Aram and Israel originally featured either Jehoahaz or Joash as the Israelite king and were only subsequently transferred to King Ahab—how might we reconstruct the redactional process that led to the texts we now have? We will follow, with some modifications and simplifications, the lead of J. Maxwell Miller, who has done the most detailed reconstruction of the redaction history of these chapters.[12] Like any other redactional hypothesis, this one is conjectural, but it accounts plausibly for the available evidence and it demonstrates well how redaction criticism reasons.

1 Kings 20 and 22: A Redaction-Critical Hypothesis

We have suggested above that the negative episodes in 20:35-43 and 22:5-28 are later expansions of stories that were originally favorable to the king of Israel featured in them, and that the older, favorable stories do not contain anything that points to prophetic circles as their originators or transmitters. On the other hand, if these stories originally concerned Joash there are *external* elements that can plausibly situate even the favorable stories in a prophetic milieu. In 2 Kings 13:14-19 the prophet Elisha is on his deathbed. He is visited by Joash, king of Israel, and he gifts the king with a last oracle that predicts three victories over Aram. The connection with Elisha assures us that this story emanates from the prophetic circles associated with him. Later the narrator informs us that the victories came to pass (13:25b) but gives no account of their happening. If 1 Kings 20 and 22 come from this period, the three battles they recount (Samaria, 20:13-21; Aphek, 20:26-30; Ramoth Gilead, 22:29-36) may well represent the three victories Elisha foretold. In that case the favorable stories in 1 Kings 20 and 22 would have been joined to each other and to the story of Elisha's death early on, if not right from the first. Prophetic circles would have transmitted this complex as part of the collection of stories about Elisha.[13] Among the

---

the throne of Israel. Unfortunately this argument is not decisive for two reasons. First, there is no reason Ahab could not have had an otherwise unmentioned son by that name. Second, there is some indication that "the king's son" describes an officer in the royal court charged with the custody of political prisoners (compare Jer 36:26; 38:6), and not necessarily a blood relative of the king.

[12] See n. 8 above, especially the article "The Elisha Cycle and the Accounts of the Omride Wars."

[13] Since the archival sources used by the Deuteronomic Historian indicate that both Jehoahaz and Joash died natural deaths ("slept with their ancestors," 2 Kgs 13:9, 13), it is possible that at this stage the story of the battle at Ramoth Gilead did not involve the king's death, but only his injury. Compare the notice of King Jehoram's injury in battle (at Ramoth

prophets, names of the kings involved would have been suppressed (if they were ever present), in order to focus attention on the figure of Elisha. This conforms to the style we see in other parts of the Elisha stories; compare, for example, the story of Elisha's cure of Naaman from leprosy (2 Kings 5), where neither the king of Israel nor the king of Aram is named.

Further modifications would have occurred over the succeeding half-century or so, and transfer of the stories to Ahab would probably have taken place later still and in a very different environment. In 722 B.C.E., the northern kingdom was conquered and destroyed by Assyrian armies under Sargon II. Refugees from the disaster fled south to the kingdom of Judah, taking with them written and oral traditions current in the north, including the prophetic stories of Elijah and Elisha and the prophecies of Hosea and Amos. In southern circles (perhaps prophetic circles and, later, Deuteronomic circles) these old stories were no longer connected, even implicitly, with any particular kings of Israel, Aram, or Judah—the last of which, of course, would have been of primary interest to Judahites. But one past king of Judah was well known to have been allied to Israel. This was Jehoshaphat, who achieved an alliance by marrying his crown prince, Joram,[14] to Athaliah, princess of the house of Omri. If the southern transmitters of the tradition decided that the anonymous king of Judah in these stories was Jehoshaphat, they would identify the anonymous king of Israel as Ahab, Jehoshaphat's contemporary.[15] The disdain in which the YHWH-alone movement held the house of Ahab[16]

Gilead!) in 2 Kings 9:14-15. Only much later, when the Israelite king's natural death had been forgotten, would the tale have been transformed (by influence from the story of Jehoram?) to include the king's death.

[14] It can be very confusing to the student that a king of Israel ("Jehoram") and a king of Judah ("Joram") with such similar names reign simultaneously. In fact, "Jehoram" and "Joram" are variant forms of the same name, and the biblical text uses them interchangeably, calling both kings "Joram" and "Jehoram" without distinction. Simply for clarity, I will impose an artificial distinction here and speak of the king of Israel as "Jehoram" and the king of Judah as "Joram."

[15] Ahab's sons, Ahaziah and Jehoram, were both also contemporaries of Jehoshaphat. But the stories of their deaths were already known (see 2 Kgs 1:2-18 and 9:21-26). So, for the Deuteronomic Historian, writing in the southern kingdom over two hundred years later, the king who died in battle at Ramoth Gilead must have been Ahab.

[16] Hatred for the house of Ahab was strong in the south as well, for good reason. Athaliah—Omrid princess and wife of Joram of Judah—is blamed by the Deuteronomic Historian for the fact that her husband "walked in the way of the kings of Israel, as the house of Ahab had done" (2 Kgs 8:18) and her son Ahaziah "walked in the way of the house of Ahab" (2 Kgs 8:26-27). Worse, after the coup d'état of Jehu resulted in the death of the kings of both Israel and Judah, Athaliah—by this time the queen mother—murdered the royal heirs (her own grandchildren!) and seized power in Jerusalem (2 Kgs 11:1). The "way of the house of Ahab" is, presumably, the worship of Baal, which was eradicated from Jerusalem as soon as Athaliah's reign came to its bloody end (2 Kgs 11:17-18).

would then account for the prophetic circles' incorporation of negative episodes (20:35-43; 22:5-28) that transform the stories from favorable to condemnatory of the king.[17] Eventually the stories would thus enter the Deuteronomic Historian's magnum opus as belonging to Ahab.

In sum, redaction criticism of the stories of Ahab's Aramean wars proves to be very complex (indeed, more complex than this sketch has shown). And it reveals a strong likelihood that the stories originally had nothing to do with Ahab at all. This means that, while they might be mined for information about one or another king of Jehu's dynasty around the turn of the eighth century B.C.E., they cannot contribute to a historical reconstruction of the life or times of King Ahab in the early ninth.

---

[17] It is impossible to determine when the story of Naboth was inserted among the stories of the Aramean wars. Most probably it happened very late, after the king of Israel in the war stories had already come to be identified as Ahab. This may help explain why, in the Greek biblical tradition (the Septuagint), the story of Naboth precedes rather than interrupts the stories of the Aramean wars.

CONCLUSION

The Construction of the King

Historical criticism seeks to retrace the history of a text's composition back to its origins, with a view to educing from the text's various stages of development whatever it can about their historical contexts. Source and redaction criticism are fundamental operations in that process. (There are others, such as form criticism and tradition history, that we have not undertaken in this study.) The questions we have pursued are only some of the issues about the Ahab traditions that warrant and reward historical critical investigation, but they enable us to construct a plausible hypothesis about the development of the figure of Ahab across the centuries during which the biblical text took shape.

King Ahab died in the mid-ninth century B.C.E. The earliest information we can retrieve, in all likelihood early enough to qualify as "contemporary or near-contemporary" with Ahab, comes from what were probably official archives of the kingdom of Israel. Ironically, this information came to be associated with the *stories* of Ahab rather late, when the Deuteronomic Historian inserted those stories into his history of the kings in the late seventh century B.C.E. These data include Ahab's accession to the throne of Israel,[1] the name of his capital, and the length of his reign (1 Kgs 16:29). Early information may also include Ahab's marriage to Jezebel of Sidon and his erection of an altar and temple to Baal and a "sacred pole" in Samaria (16:31b-33a). It is less certain, however, that this

---

[1] Actually the correlation of Ahab's accession year with the reign of the corresponding king in Judah is problematic, because the ancient Hebrew and Greek traditions disagree on this point. Presumably one of the two preserves the archival information unchanged and the other has been modified in the process of transmission, but it is not possible to tell which is which. See n. 8, p. 91.

comes unmodified from archival sources, since the hand of the Deutero-nomic Historian is evident in the negative assessment of Ahab that surrounds this information (16:31a, 33b). Quite likely the notice about Hiel's recon-struction of Jericho comes from the archival material—it is hard to imag-ine why the Deuteronomic Historian would include it otherwise, since it plays no role anywhere else in his account of Ahab's reign. Finally, the for-mulaic notices about Ahab's death from natural causes ("slept with his an-cestors," 22:40) and the succession of his son Ahaziah also probably derive from the archival material.

Within prophetic circles stories of various prophets, named and un-named, circulated as a way of celebrating memorable colleagues of the past. At the same time, in those same circles, a movement was developing to promote exclusive worship of YHWH and to oppose a polytheist practice that would worship YHWH along with, even though supreme over, other deities. Such seems to have been the accepted practice of the time, and the prophetic insistence on exclusive worship of YHWH appears to be an inno-vation in the ninth century. It is understandable, then, that the prophetic tra-ditions handed on in these circles would also incorporate a polemic against the worship of other gods, and in particular against the worship of Baal, the most widely revered Canaanite god. Supporters of exclusive Yahwism would have seen an inclusive polytheistic system as infidelity to YHWH and would have condemned any royal cooperation in such a system, including Ahab's building of a temple for Baal in Samaria.

There is some indication that, during the reign of Ahab or his two sons, an event occurred in which a serious injustice was perpetrated against an Israelite landowner (Naboth). The injustice was laid to the account of the royal house, though it is not certain whether the king involved was Ahab or one of his sons. There is also evidence of military support for a change of régime during the reign of Ahab's son Jehoram.

All together this points to a growing anti-Ahab (or anti-house of Ahab) sentiment in the years leading up to Jehu's coup d'état around 842 B.C.E. Such a context would be fertile ground for the development of stories hos-tile to reigning members of the house of Ahab as well as to its eponymous ancestor. Such stories may have developed as part of a resistance movement before the coup, or as justification for the coup after it had taken place. This could account for the combination of stories of Ahab and the drought with polemical anti-Baal stories in 1 Kings 18, and for some early version of the Naboth incident—though, in the latter case, that version may not have been identical with what we now have in 1 Kings 21:1-16.

During the century-long course of the Jehu dynasty the existing sto-ries of Ahab would have undergone relatively little radical change—

perhaps some intensification, perhaps some shift in *dramatis personae* from a son of Ahab to Ahab himself. At the same time, stories about Jehu's descendants and their on-again, off-again wars with Aram developed and, within prophetic circles associated with Elisha, became stories about his prophetic ministry during the reign of an unnamed king of Israel.

After the fall of Samaria to the Assyrians, northern traditions came south to Judah with Israelite refugees. In southern circles the identification of the fundamental evil of the house of Ahab as promotion of Baalism would have strengthened under the impetus of popular hatred for Athaliah, the queen mother who usurped the throne after the death of her son Ahaziah. Her Israelite origins, her connections with the house of Ahab, and her support of Baalism in Jerusalem would have fueled the antipathy of exclusive Yahwists for anything having to do with Ahab's memory. At the same time, southern transmitters of the originally northern stories of Elisha would have attempted to fit those stories into what they knew of their own history. An alliance between a king of Israel and a king of Judah, for these southern tradents, would almost automatically point back to the Omrid period, when Jehoshaphat of Judah achieved an alliance with Israel by marrying Athaliah of Israel to his own son Joram. The stories of the Aramean war were therefore identified as belonging to the period of this alliance because of the entente they depict between Judah and Israel: The king of Judah was identified as Jehoshaphat and the king of Israel as his contemporary Ahab.

But since the stories of the Aramean wars portrayed the king of Israel in positive light they were expanded in the prophetic circles of the south by the addition of episodes that cast strong condemnatory shadows on that king, now understood to be the heinous Baalist Ahab. In this form they eventually reached the hands of the Deuteronomic Historian late in the seventh century B.C.E.[2] From the disparate materials he received—archival records, prophetic traditions, etc.—he fashioned an account of Ahab's reign that reflected his own theological commitments to exclusive Yahwism. As seen by the Deuteronomic Historian, Ahab "did evil in the sight of YHWH more than all who were before him" (1 Kgs 16:30; see also 16:33b).

---

[2] The history of the Deuteronomic redactions is a continuing matter for debate among biblical scholars. It is generally agreed that the Deuteronomic History as a unified work (that is, the books of Joshua, Judges, 1–2 Samuel, and 1–2 Kings) went through at least two editions, and that at least the final edition was achieved during the Babylonian Exile. It is possible that some or all of the Ahab stories did not enter the History in the first edition (late seventh century B.C.E.) but in a later one.

CONCLUSION
Of Methods and Meanings

OF METHODS
AND MEANINGS

We have explored several different ways of reading the biblical passages that tell us of King Ahab. Each approach has produced a strikingly disparate result. Historical inference from the very sparse, probably reliable data we possess produces a minimal sketch with little detail. Ahab appears to be the typical ninth-century B.C.E. monarch of a small but prosperous pocket kingdom on the Levantine coast. Along with other nearby kingdoms, he is faced with the threat of a giant, brutal, and expansionist Assyria, and along with them he withstands the giant with some success. He dies a natural death and his son succeeds him.

Narrative criticism of the character of Ahab in 1 Kings 16–22 paints a much darker picture. Ahab is a religious apostate, offering both passive and active support to the worship of Baal over against the worship of YHWH, the God of Israel, condoning (if not instigating) the judicial murder of an innocent landowner, frequently dismissive of YHWH's will as expressed by prophets, and ultimately tricked and trapped by YHWH and killed in battle. His son succeeds him.

Historical criticism enables us to see how stories about Ahab might have developed over time to transform the memories of the historical king into the dark, negative narrative portrait we have in the present text. But in working out such an explanation, source and redaction criticisms inevitably point up sharply the stark difference between our biblical account and a reasonable historical reconstruction. How are we to contend with this difference? If the text does not offer us reliable history, then what does it offer?

The dilemma is still thornier when one recognizes that both historical criticism and narrative criticism begin with the same text and, in great measure, base their reasoning on identical observations about the text. It will not have escaped the careful student that narrative criticism's identification of several "narrators" and historical criticism's identification of several "redactors" are both based on the same sorts of tensions in the text and that they come to analogous conclusions, namely, that the tensions are to be explained by a plurality of viewpoints embedded in the text. Where narrative criticism locates that plurality within the narrative world, historical criticism locates it in the primary world of the real author and reader. The difference is due not to the nature of the fundamental observations, but to the goals and presuppositions of the respective methods.

Narrative criticism commits itself to meaning that can be discerned within the text. It *chooses* to read the text *as if* it were a unitary composition, whether it is or not. To put it in literary terms, it posits an "implied author," a single and singular creative wellspring for the entire text. It does not claim (or deny) that that source of unity exists, or ever existed, in the real world; it simply takes as a starting point that the text *can* be read as a unified whole with coherent meaning and that, therefore, for this to be possible we must be able to speak—at least metaphorically—of an "author." From a literary perspective this means that the "implied author" exists *outside* the narrative world he creates, but *inside* the text that evidences his existence.

Our earlier diagram, then, becomes somewhat more complex. The "implied author" is the set of intentions and values we must assume in order to read the text as a coherent unity; the "implied reader" is the set of

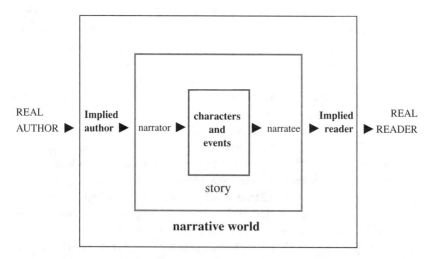

(Based on Terence J. Keegan, *Interpreting the Bible: A Popular Introduction to Biblical Hermeneutics* [New York: Paulist, 1985] 94.)

abilities and attitudes the text presumes in a reader in order to be understood perfectly. Both are outside the narrative because they do not function within the economy of narrator and narratee; both are inside the text because they are wholly constructed *by the reader* from the evidence of the text itself. So narrative criticism's quest, ideally, remains always within the text, and seeks to identify the "meaning" the "implied author" wishes to communicate to the "implied reader."

Historical criticism works from different presuppositions. It allows that the compositional process may have produced a text that does not cohere perfectly—the vagaries of transmission, haphazard as they are, may well have resulted in false starts and loose ends, *non sequiturs* and irresolvable conflicts. It is interested in reconstructing the real author(s), historical contexts, and social functions that lie behind the text and its complexities; and so its methods concentrate on the disparate and contingent historical factors that influenced the gradual shaping of the final text rather than on a coherent "meaning" presupposed to be contained in it. The result is a multitude of "authors," each of whose texts was intended to communicate a distinct "meaning," and their manifold witness to historical realities overshadows any ultimate "meaning" that may have been generated from their eventual fusion.

A text, like any other human artifact, can be a source of many types of knowledge as long as we ask the right questions. A painting, for example, can tell us something of how the artist understands a particular aspect of reality. But it could also tell us something about artistic (or perhaps religious, or political, or social) conventions in the artist's day, or about the weathering of pigments through the years, and so forth. If we ask the right historical questions of a text, as historical criticism attempts, we may succeed in retrieving historical information. If we ask narrative questions, we will not. Conversely, narrative questions can reveal the sort of universal human truths proper to art that no amount of historical questioning can ever attain. Both searches are worthwhile and can yield rich treasure.

In the last analysis the search for *original* (i.e., historical) meaning and the search for *textual* (i.e., literary) meaning are different quests. They require different critical methods and they reach incommensurable goals. The type of questions we ask—in other words, the interpretive methods we employ—will in part control which goal we reach and what sort of truth we find there. Far from being an indication that the search for meaning is hopeless, this should be a reminder to us of the inexhaustible richness of the biblical text.

GENERAL INDEX

Note: **bold-face** page numbers indicate more substantive treatments of the subject.

Fredenburg, Brandon L., 39 n. 10,
91 n. 9

golden calf, *see* "Jeroboam, sin of"
Gray, John, 107 n. 8

Hadad-ezer of Aram (Damascus), 5,
105, 107
Hamilton, Jeffries M., 72 n. 66
Hazael of Aram (Damascus), 6, 32
ḥesed, 41–42
Hiel of Bethel, 22–23
historical criticism, 119
House of David Inscription, *see* "Tel
Dan Inscription"

idolatry, 60, 62, 64, 79; *see also* "Baal
and Baalism," "Jeroboam, sin of"
implied author, 34 n. 1, 118–119
implied reader, 118–119
indirect showing, *see* "characterization"
inheritance, ancestral, 49–53
interior monologue, *see* "internal
monologue"
internal monologue, 19 n. 5, 50
Irhuleni of Hamath, 5 n. 3
Ittobaal of Sidon, *see* "Ethbaal of
Sidon"
ivories, Samarian, 8, 76, 91

Jackson, Kent P., 6 n. 4
Jahaz, 6
Jehoram of Israel, 6, 96 n. 11, 99,
109 n. 15
Jehoshaphat of Judah, 65, 67, 109
Jehu of Israel, 4 n. 2, 6 n. 5, 32, 99,
102
Jepsen, Alfred, 107
Jericho, 32, 46 n. 24, 76 n. 71
Jeroboam I of Israel, 56–57
Jeroboam, sin of, 21, 29, 57, 62, 79
Jeroboam, way of, *see* "Jeroboam,
sin of"
Jezebel, 22, 32, 50–53, 58–60, 62–64,
79, 97–99

Jezreel, 48
Joash of Israel, 108
Joram of Judah, 109

Keegan, Terence J., 13, 118
Kelle, Brad, 4 n. 2

Long, Burke O., 20 n. 7
Long, Jesse C., Jr., 57 n. 46
"lord" (as translation), 67 n. 58

Mesha of Moab, 5–6
Mesha Stele, 5–6
messenger formula, 36, 54, 57,
72 n. 65
Micaiah ben Imlah, 70–75, 101–102
Miller, J. Maxwell, 98 n. 14, 107 n. 8,
108
Moabite Stone, *see* "Mesha Stele"
money, 49 n. 29
monolatry, 96
Monolith Inscription, 5, 105, 107
monologue, interior, *see* "internal
monologue"
monologue, internal, *see* "internal
monologue"
monotheism, 95–96
Moses and Moses traditions, 30–31

Naboth, 49
Napier, Davie, 55 n. 41
narratee, 13–14
narrative criticism, **13–20, 33–35,** 118
narrative voice, *see* "narrator"
narrative world, 13–16
narrator, 13–14, **16–18, 33–35,** 58–59,
60–63, 74–79
Naveh, Joseph, 7 n. 6

Obadiah, 20, 26, 55, 97 n. 12
O'Brien, Mark A., 92 n. 1
Omri of Israel, 4–9, 21

point of view, 17–18
Polzin, Robert M., 16 n. 4
Provan, Iain W., 39 n. 10

INDEX OF
SCRIPTURAL REFERENCES

Note: **bold-face** page numbers indicate more substantial treatments of the passage.